I0518852

When They're Talking About You

Finding Healing After Character Attacks

Lea Cole

Copyright © 2025 Lea Cole All rights reserved.

No part of this publication may be reproduced, distributed, or transmitted in any form or by any means, including photocopying, recording, or other electronic or mechanical methods, without the prior written permission of the author, except in the case of brief quotations embodied in critical reviews and certain other noncommercial uses permitted by copyright law.

For permission requests, contact the author at leacoleauthor@gmail.com

ISBN: 979-8-9934193-0-5

First Edition

Published in the United States of America

Scripture Permissions:

All Scripture quotations marked (NIV) are taken from the Holy Bible, New International Version®, NIV®. Copyright ©1973, 1978, 1984, 2011 by Biblica, Inc.™ Used by permission of Zondervan. All rights reserved worldwide.

All Scripture quotations marked (NLT) are taken from the Holy Bible, New Living Translation, copyright ©1996, 2004, 2015 by Tyndale House Foundation. Used by permission of Tyndale House Publishers, Carol Stream, Illinois 60188. All rights reserved.

Disclaimer:

The content in this book is for informational and inspirational purposes. While the author has made every effort to provide accurate and helpful information, this book is not intended as a substitute for professional counseling, therapy, or medical advice. Readers are encouraged to seek appropriate professional help when needed.

Table of Contents

Introduction

You never expect it to happen to you.

One day you're excited about a new position, eager to contribute and build relationships. The next, you're walking into rooms where conversations stop, watching colleagues exchange glances you can't decode, and wondering if the isolation you feel is real or just your imagination.

It's real. And if you're reading this book, you probably know that now.

But here's what you might not know yet: this isn't the end of your story. The isolation you're feeling right now, the confusion about what went wrong, the questions about your own sanity—these are not your final destination. They're the beginning of a journey that can transform you into someone stronger, wiser, and anchored in unshakeable truth.

Whether it happened in a workplace, church, family system, or community organization, the experience of being targeted by sustained gossip feels unlike anything else. It's not just hurt feelings or wounded pride—it's the systematic dismantling of your reputation, relationships, and sense of reality by people who smile to your face while undermining you behind your back.

The questions come fast and relentless: What did I do wrong? How did this start? Why won't it stop? Who can I trust? Am I losing my mind? Is this really happening, or am I being paranoid? Does God see what's happening to me?

This book was born from those questions and the painful education that followed—not just surviving the experience of malicious gossip, but understanding the deeper dynamics at play and discovering the tools that actually work for protection, healing, and moving forward.

Why This Book Matters Now

We live in a culture where information travels faster than truth, where social media amplifies whispers into roars, and where character assassination has become an acceptable form of conflict. Gossip isn't just idle chatter anymore, it's weaponized communication that destroys careers, relationships, and communities with unprecedented speed and reach.

Yet most of us are unprepared for these attacks. We expect basic fairness, direct communication, and the assumption of good intentions. We expect that doing good work and treating people well will protect us from malicious targeting. We expect organizations and communities to have systems in place that prevent or address toxic behavior.

Too often, these expectations are shattered.

Digital platforms have given gossip new weapons that previous generations couldn't imagine. Group texts and private message chains become breeding grounds for character assassination. Screenshots live forever. Today's trusted friend becomes tomorrow's prosecutor. The damage spreads exponentially, often before targets even realize they're under attack.

Meanwhile, the spiritual and emotional toll of being misunderstood, isolated, and attacked cuts deeper than most people realize. Beyond damaged reputations and awkward social dynamics lies real trauma—betrayal of trust, powerlessness against lies, and the soul-crushing realization that some people will destroy your peace without a second thought.

Who This Book Is For

If you're reading this because you've been blindsided by malicious gossip in any area of your life, you'll find practical strategies for protecting your mental health, maintaining your integrity, and responding with wisdom rather than reactivity. You'll learn how to recognize early warning signs, build boundaries that actually work, and avoid getting pulled into toxic dynamics.

If you're a leader in any capacity—whether in business, ministry, education, or community organizations—you'll discover how to identify and address gossip before it poisons your culture. Leadership failures often enable gossip campaigns and destroy organizational health, but strong leadership can create environments where healthy communication flourishes.

If you've ever participated in gossip and felt the sting of conviction afterward, you'll find a path toward healthier communication patterns that build relationships instead of destroying them. Understanding the true cost of gossip isn't just about avoiding harm—it's about choosing to speak life instead of death.

If you're simply tired of navigating environments where whispers hold more power than truth, this book offers hope. It's possible to create gossip-free zones. It's possible to heal from the damage. It's possible to build something better.

A Faith-Based Approach to Real-World Problems

This book approaches gossip and character assassination through the lens of biblical wisdom while addressing the practical realities of surviving these attacks in any environment. You don't need to share my faith to benefit from the strategies and insights contained here, but understanding God's heart for healthy communication and His promises of protection provides an anchor that human wisdom alone cannot supply.

Scripture doesn't minimize the pain of betrayal or the challenge of loving difficult people. The Psalms are full of cries for justice and protection from those who "sharpen their tongues like swords and aim cruel words like deadly arrows" (Psalm 64:3). But God's Word also provides the path through suffering to strength, through pain to purpose, through confusion to clarity.

This journey isn't about positive thinking or quick fixes. It's about discovering whose voice you'll follow when everything feels chaotic—the voice of fear, anger, and human opinion, or the voice of truth, love, and divine purpose.

A Note About the Stories in This Book

The principles and strategies in this book are drawn from real experiences and situations, though details have been carefully altered to protect privacy and maintain confidentiality. My personal story forms the foundation, but specific circumstances, timelines, and identifying details have been changed.

The additional characters and scenarios you'll encounter—like Rebecca's family dynamics or workplace situations—represent composite examples that illustrate common patterns many people experience. These stories combine elements from multiple real situations to demonstrate authentic dynamics while protecting everyone involved.

What matters isn't whether you encounter someone exactly like the people described, but whether you recognize the underlying patterns and learn strategies that work in your unique situation. The conversations and scenarios reflect genuine dynamics, even when specific details serve illustrative rather than documentary purposes.

The core truth remains constant: gossip causes real damage, healing is possible, and there are practical steps that actually work for protection and recovery. These examples serve to make those truths accessible and applicable to your circumstances.

What You'll Discover

This book will take you through a complete journey of understanding, survival, and recovery:

You'll learn to recognize gossip in all its disguises and how innocent sharing can progress into character assassination, from "concerns" to digital group messages that build cases against absent people. Understanding these tactics is the first step in protecting yourself.

You'll discover how to respond wisely when attacks begin, moving beyond reactive defensiveness to strategic wisdom that protects your peace while maintaining your integrity.

You'll build the spiritual and emotional resilience needed for extended battles, learning practical tools for maintaining your strength when human solutions feel inadequate.

You'll create practical boundaries that protect your healing without isolating you from healthy relationships, learning the difference between wisdom and withdrawal.

You'll find peace that doesn't depend on perfect circumstances or others' approval—the deep, abiding peace that remains steady regardless of external chaos.

You'll understand how leadership either enables toxic cultures or creates environments where healthy communication thrives, whether you're currently in authority or preparing for future opportunities.

You'll work through the challenging process of forgiveness and healing, learning to release those who hurt you while protecting yourself from further harm.

Finally, you'll learn how to step boldly into your future, no longer defined by what was done to you but empowered by who you've become through the healing process.

Your Story Doesn't End Here

If you're in the middle of a gossip attack right now, reading this while feeling isolated, confused, and overwhelmed, let me offer you hope:

this is not the end of your story. What feels like destruction is often preparation. What seems like an ending is often a beginning.

The confidence you'll build through surviving this trial will be tested and proven. The discernment you'll develop will serve you for the rest of your life. The compassion you'll gain for others facing similar struggles will become a bridge to relationships and opportunities you can't yet imagine.

Others' opinions are not your reality. Their voices do not get to write your story's conclusion.

This transformation—from someone under attack to someone walking in strength and purpose—is what these pages hold. You have more strength than you know, more support than you can see, and more purpose than your pain has allowed you to remember.

Let's begin this journey together. Your healing starts here.

Chapter 1: The Moment Everything Changed

Two years ago, I thought my career was over. I'd wake up with dread pooling in my stomach, wondering if today would be the day they'd finally find an excuse to let me go. I questioned everything—my competence, my character, even my sanity. The workplace I'd entered with such excitement had become a battlefield I never saw coming.

Today, I'm stronger, wiser, and moving forward with confidence I never had before. The discernment I developed during that trial serves me daily. The compassion I gained for others facing similar struggles has opened doors to relationships and opportunities I couldn't have imagined. But the journey between those two points taught me everything I know about surviving workplace toxicity and emerging victorious.

That transformation didn't happen overnight. The path began in what seemed like an ideal situation, a new job that checked off so many important boxes.

When Everything Started to Unravel

The company had an impressive reputation, the role aligned perfectly with my skills, and the salary offered financial stability I'd been working toward for years. When colleagues casually invited me out for drinks during my first week, I accepted without hesitation, eager to build relationships with my new team.

That evening became my first glimpse into dynamics I didn't yet understand. Instead of casual getting-to-know-you conversation, I found myself listening to a systematic dissection of other team members, their flaws, shortcomings, and daily approaches to work. Nothing seemed off-limits for criticism. Different colleagues were picked apart with calculated precision, their mistakes catalogued, their motives questioned.

As the new person, I had no intention of getting involved. I smiled politely, changed the subject when possible, and made a mental note to keep my distance from office drama. But even as I tried to stay neutral, I was absorbing a troubling reality: this wasn't just casual workplace venting. This was something more deliberate and pervasive.

Over the following weeks, a clearer picture emerged. I had stepped into a toxic dynamic where certain individuals wielded influence like weapons, creating divisions within our small team. Leadership seemed unaware that their own participation in negative discussions about absent colleagues was poisoning the work environment like a slow leak of carbon monoxide.

The environment operated on an unspoken rule: someone refuses to join the insider group's campaigns against others, and they become the next target. Once it became clear I wouldn't participate in gossip about other team members, the focus shifted to me.

Information gaps appeared where I should have been included. Alliance behaviors became obvious as certain people consistently supported each other while subtly undermining me. Discussions about my work, my attitude, and my "fit" with the team began spreading beyond our department to other areas of the company.

The isolation was unlike anything I had experienced—calculated, persistent, and designed to make me question my own perceptions. By the time I understood the full scope of the campaign, narratives about me had spread to places where I had no relationships to counter the false impressions being created.

The Crisis Deepens

The situation escalated when I realized my job performance evaluations were being influenced by these dynamics. Projects I had completed successfully were being questioned. My communication style was being characterized as problematic. My ability to be a "team player" was suddenly under scrutiny, despite my consistent efforts to support colleagues and contribute positively.

After more than a year of enduring this treatment, I faced a choice: leave defeated or stay and fight for my integrity. I chose to stay, but not in my own strength. I leaned into God, trusting His guidance through the storm. The very discernment He provided became my anchor and my guide for navigating the challenges ahead.

Through this painful season, I discovered that God could use even the most destructive situation to develop character, wisdom, and resilience I never knew I needed. The confidence I built through surviving this trial has been tested and proven in countless situations since. The skills I learned for recognizing and responding to toxic dynamics have served me in every area of life.

Most surprisingly, the experience that nearly broke me became the foundation for helping others facing similar battles. God transformed what was meant for destruction into purpose.

The Deeper Learning

The dynamics I witnessed taught me something profound about the nature of gossip that I had never understood before. I had thought of gossip as casual, temporary, and relatively harmless—something that hurt in the moment but eventually faded away like a bruise. I discovered that gossip could be weaponized and used as a tool of professional and personal destruction with devastating effectiveness.

The impact ran deeper than damaged reputation or workplace awkwardness. It was about the betrayal of trust, the powerlessness of watching narratives take on lives of their own, and the soul-crushing realization that some people will destroy your peace without a second thought.

But it was also about discovering that God sees every whispered word and hidden motive. That His justice, while sometimes delayed, is always perfect. That experiences meant to end your story can become the beginning of a new chapter if you let Him write what comes next.

That experience forced me to ask questions I had never considered before: How does gossip actually spread and gain power? Why do some people weaponize it while others refuse to participate? How do certain environments become toxic breeding grounds for malicious talk while others remain healthy? How do you protect yourself when you become the target? And most importantly, how do you heal from the damage and emerge stronger than before?

Your Journey Forward

This book emerged from that painful education and the discovery that survival isn't enough—true healing requires understanding the deeper dynamics at play and learning tools that actually work for protection and recovery.

The experience that challenged my sense of self and tested my resilience became the foundation for helping others navigate similar battles. What was meant for harm, God transformed into purpose and wisdom that can serve anyone facing the devastating effects of character assassination.

The journey ahead will take you from confusion to clarity, from reactive survival to strategic wisdom, from isolation to genuine community. You'll discover that your current pain has purpose and that healing is not only possible but promised to those who trust God through the process.

Understanding the real cost of gossip's destruction is where we begin. When you see what's truly at stake, you'll understand why the battle is worth fighting and why the victory is so sweet.

Chapter 2: The Real Cost: What Gossip Actually Destroys

When we talk about the damage gossip causes, we often focus on hurt feelings or wounded pride. But the destruction runs far deeper than momentary embarrassment or social awkwardness. Gossip doesn't just sting—it systematically dismantles the very foundations that healthy relationships and communities are built upon.

God's design for human connection is rooted in truth, love, and trust. Proverbs 11:13 warns that "a gossip betrays a confidence, but a trustworthy person keeps a secret". This isn't just about keeping information private—it's about understanding that when we break confidence, we're tearing at the fabric of what makes relationships possible.

That's gossip's goal. But here's what gossip doesn't tell you: skilled architects can rebuild from ashes, and the new structure often surpasses what was there before.

The Wrecking Ball: How Trust Dies

Trust is the currency of all relationships. It's built slowly, brick by brick, through consistent actions and words that prove someone is safe to be vulnerable with. You know those relationships where you can say anything without fear? Where you don't have to edit or perform? That's trust at work.

Gossip doesn't just damage trust—it obliterates it with the efficiency of a wrecking ball.

When gossip infiltrates any environment, people start editing themselves. They withhold not just secrets but genuine thoughts, struggles, and ideas. The very openness that allows relationships to deepen becomes dangerous. Suddenly, everyone's walking on eggshells, calculating every word, wondering what's safe to share.

But trust that survives betrayal and emerges stronger creates bonds that are nearly unbreakable. When people see someone maintain their character under pressure, it creates a level of respect that surface-level interactions never achieve.

Gossip is the kindling that keeps conflicts burning and suspicion growing. When we remove it, peace has space to flourish and trust can begin its patient work of reconstruction.

The Ripple Effect: When One Stone Hits Still Water

Have you ever thrown a stone into a perfectly calm lake? That splash isn't the end of the story—it's just the beginning. Ripples spread outward in ever-widening circles, reaching shores the stone never touched.

Gossip works the same way, but here's what I've learned: positive change creates ripples too. When one person chooses integrity over gossip, when one leader addresses toxic dynamics, when one family member refuses to participate in character assassination, those choices also spread in widening circles.

Entire communities suffer when gossip becomes normalized. Churches may see congregants stop sharing prayer requests because they know it might become next week's "concern." Neighborhoods can split into factions over rumors that started with one person's misunderstanding. Workplace productivity drops as people spend energy navigating toxic dynamics instead of focusing on their actual work.

The ripple effect extends to people who weren't even present when the gossip occurred. Future relationships become more difficult because targets may struggle with trust issues. New employees, church members, or neighbors inherit the tension and divided loyalties created by past gossip, stepping into environments poisoned by conflicts they had no part in creating.

But I've also seen communities that address gossip directly emerge stronger and more unified than they were before the crisis. The courage to confront toxic dynamics creates new ripples of health that spread just as far as the original damage—often farther.

When Your Name Becomes a Weapon

Your reputation is more than what people think about you, it's your ability to move freely in the world, to build new relationships, to contribute meaningfully to your community. It's your calling card, your introduction before you even speak.

Gossip doesn't just damage reputation; when it's malicious, it can completely assassinate someone's ability to start fresh or rebuild.

The insidious nature of gossip means that by the time you realize your reputation is under attack, the damage has often spread beyond your ability to contain it. People form judgments based on fragments of information, assumptions, and secondhand accounts. Truth becomes irrelevant when the narrative has already taken hold.

This is why Proverbs 22:1 reminds us that "a good name is more desirable than great riches; to be esteemed is better than silver or gold". When gossip destroys a good name, it's stealing something more valuable than material possessions, it's stealing someone's ability to be received with openness and goodwill.

I remember walking into meetings and seeing the subtle shift in people's faces, not hostility exactly, but caution. Colleagues who had never worked directly with me, who knew nothing about my character or contributions, had formed opinions based entirely on whispered conversations and assumptions. My reputation preceded me into every interaction, coloring how my words were received and my actions interpreted.

It was like trying to introduce yourself while wearing a disguise you didn't know you had on.

But here's what I've learned: character assassinations don't always succeed permanently against people of genuine integrity. Truth has a persistent way of surfacing, often when least expected and in ways that vindicate more powerfully than any defense could have achieved.

The Mind Under Siege

Being the target of sustained gossip creates a unique form of psychological torture. Unlike direct confrontation, which can be addressed and resolved, gossip operates in shadows. You can't defend against accusations you're not aware of or confront people who smile to your face while undermining you behind your back.

But there's hope even in this area. The mind that has been under siege can be renewed, and the peace that comes from surviving gossip attacks is unlike any other peace you'll experience.

The constant vigilance required to navigate a gossip-infected environment is exhausting. You find yourself analyzing every interaction, wondering what was really meant, questioning your own perceptions. Sleep becomes elusive when your mind won't stop replaying conversations. Concentration suffers when part of your mental energy is constantly scanning for threats.

Some individuals develop a "gossip radar," a heightened awareness that remains active even after they have left a toxic environment. For others, this experience fosters discernment. What the enemy meant as a wound becomes a gift that protects not just them, but everyone they have the privilege to influence.

The Wounds That Don't Show

Perhaps the most insidious aspect of gossip's destruction is the damage that remains hidden beneath the surface, affecting victims long after the immediate crisis has passed.

Self-doubt becomes a constant companion during gossip attacks. You start second-guessing your own perceptions, wondering if you somehow deserved the treatment you received, questioning your judgment about people and situations. The gaslighting effect of gossip creates lasting confusion about your own instincts and experiences.

I found myself asking questions I'd never asked before: Am I really as difficult as they're saying? Maybe I'm too sensitive. Perhaps I don't read situations well. Do I even fit in here?

The ability to form new relationships becomes compromised when trust has been broken by gossip's betrayal. Professional development may stagnate as victims become reluctant to take risks or put themselves in visible positions where they might become targets again.

Spiritual struggles emerge as victims wrestle with questions about God's protection, justice, and their own worth in His eyes. Where was God when this was happening? Why didn't He stop it?

But these questions, while painful, often lead to a faith that is tested, proven, and unshakeable. The self-examination forced by crisis ultimately strengthens character and clarifies calling. People emerge with enhanced ability to form deeper, more authentic relationships, having learned to distinguish between surface-level connections and people of genuine character.

When Communities Fracture

Healthy communities are built on shared values, mutual respect, and the assumption that members will treat each other with basic dignity. When gossip infiltrates these environments, it changes the entire culture. People stop assuming good intentions. Collaboration becomes difficult when trust is scarce. New members sense the tension even if they can't identify its source.

The cost extends to future generations as children who grow up in environments where gossip is common learn that this is how relationships work. They model what they see, carrying toxic communication patterns into their own relationships and communities.

Communities that address gossip directly can emerge stronger and more unified than they were before the crisis. The courage to confront toxic dynamics creates environments where honest conversation replaces whispered complaints, and diverse groups learn to navigate disagreements with grace.

The Spiritual Battlefield

Perhaps the most devastating cost of gossip is its spiritual impact— both on those who spread it and those who suffer from it. Gossip creates division where God desires unity, breeds judgment where He calls for grace, and destroys the very community that reflects His heart.

For those who participate in gossip, there's often a gradual hardening of the heart. As Proverbs 4:23 reminds us, "Above all else, guard your heart, for everything you do flows from it." When we allow gossip to take root, it corrupts the wellspring of our actions and words.

For targets of gossip, the spiritual damage often manifests as questions about God's protection and justice. Faith can be shaken when it feels like those who spread lies prosper while those who seek to live with integrity suffer.

But here's what I know: God sees every whispered word and hidden motive. Nothing escapes His notice, and His justice, though sometimes it feels delayed, is always perfect and often exceeds what we could have asked or imagined.

The Hope Beyond the Wreckage

Understanding these costs isn't meant to overwhelm you, it's meant to open your eyes to what's truly at stake and motivate you to fight for what can be restored. When you see the real price of gossip, you understand why God takes it so seriously and why the battle for restoration is worth fighting.

God's heart is always toward restoration. What gossip seeks to destroy, His love can rebuild. What lies have torn down, His truth can restore. I've seen it happen—reputations rebuilt stronger than before, relationships restored with deeper intimacy, communities healed and transformed, and individuals who emerge from the valley with wisdom, strength, and purpose they never had before the attack.

The cost of gossip is high, but the hope of restoration is higher still. The journey from destruction to healing begins with understanding what's truly at stake and believing that what God promises to rebuild will surpass what was lost.

In recognizing the warning signs that we'll explore next, you're taking the first step toward protecting what matters most and beginning the journey toward the restoration that awaits on the other side of this battle.

Chapter 3: Recognizing Gossip in All Its Forms

Understanding the true cost of gossip's destruction naturally leads to an urgent question: How do we recognize it before it takes root? After experiencing firsthand how devastating malicious gossip can be, I became a student of its various disguises. What I discovered surprised me: gossip rarely announces itself with a neon sign saying "malicious rumor ahead!" Instead, it hides behind concern, disguises itself as spiritual care, and dresses itself up as legitimate conversation.

The Bible warns us to be wise as serpents and innocent as doves (Matthew 10:16). Part of that wisdom involves understanding how deception operates so we can guard against it. This isn't about becoming paranoid or suspicious of every conversation, it's about developing the discernment that protects ourselves and others from subtle attacks on character and community.

What Is Gossip, Really?

Before we explore gossip's many disguises, we need a clear definition of what we're dealing with. The Hebrew word for gossip, *rakil*, literally means "to go about as a talebearer" or "merchant of secrets." It paints the picture of someone who trades in other people's private information like a merchant trades in goods—for personal profit or gain.

Gossip isn't just any conversation about another person—it's the sharing of information about someone who isn't present, particularly when that information is:

- **Unverified or speculative** - "I think maybe..." or "I heard that..."

- **Shared without permission** - private information that wasn't yours to distribute

- **Unnecessary for the listener to know** - details that don't help them pray, help, or understand a situation they're directly involved in

- **Potentially damaging** - information that could harm someone's reputation or relationships

- **Shared with wrong motives** - entertainment, bonding through criticism, or building a case against someone

Scripture makes clear distinctions about our speech. Ephesians 4:29 instructs us: "Do not let any unwholesome talk come out of your mouths, but only what is helpful for building others up according to their needs, that it may benefit those who listen". This verse provides a powerful filter for our conversations: Does this build up? Does it benefit the listener? Does it meet a genuine need?

Not every conversation about an absent person constitutes gossip. Legitimate sharing includes:

- **Necessary information** - "Abigail's mom is in the hospital, so she might need extra support this week"

- **Public information** - "Did you see John got promoted? That's wonderful!"

- **Seeking wisdom** - "I'm having a conflict with a colleague. Can you help me think through how to approach this biblically?" (without unnecessary personal details)

- **Protective warnings** - "I need to let you know about a concerning pattern I've witnessed" (shared appropriately with those who need to know)

The Psalms repeatedly address the power of words and the damage caused by those who "sharpen their tongues like swords and aim cruel words like deadly arrows" (Psalm 64:3).

The distinction often lies not in the content but in the heart behind the sharing. Proverbs 16:28 warns that "a perverse person stirs up conflict, and a gossip separates close friends". When our words divide rather than unite, when they tear down rather than build up, we've crossed from legitimate sharing into gossip's territory.

Jesus Himself addressed the heart issue behind our words: "For the mouth speaks what the heart is full of. A good man brings good things out of the good stored up in him, and an evil man brings evil things out of the evil stored up in him" (Matthew 12:34-35). Our conversations about others reveal what's really in our hearts—love and concern, or something darker.

The Slippery Slope: How Innocent Sharing Becomes Malicious Gossip

One of gossip's most dangerous characteristics is how gradually it progresses from innocent sharing to character assassination. Like a cancer, it starts small and spreads, often without the participants realizing how far they've traveled from their original intentions.

Understanding this progression helps us recognize when we're beginning to slide down the slope—and catch ourselves before we reach the bottom.

Stage 1: The Innocent Observation

It often begins with something genuinely innocent: "I noticed Tom seemed really stressed during the meeting today." Scripture affirms that caring observation is natural and even godly. Galatians 6:2 instructs us to "carry each other's burdens, and in this way you will fulfill the law of Christ". The danger lies in what happens next. If we stop here and follow up with direct care, we stay in healthy territory. But if the observation becomes the opening line of a deeper conversation, we've taken the first step down the slope that

Proverbs 18:8 warns about: "The words of a gossip are like choice morsels; they go down to the inmost parts".

Stage 2: The Connecting of Dots

The next stage involves connecting observations into theories: "Tom seemed really stressed, and he's been leaving work early a lot lately. I wonder if he's having problems at home." Now we've moved from observation to speculation, from facts to assumptions. This is where many well-meaning people lose their footing. Deuteronomy 19:15 establishes that "a matter must be established by the testimony of two or three witnesses"—but here we're building cases on assumptions rather than witness testimony.

Stage 3: The Information Gathering

Once a theory is formed, the next progression is gathering more information: "Have you noticed Tom leaving early? Do you know what's going on with him?" This transforms passive observation into active investigation. The person may still believe their motives are pure, but they've now recruited others into speculation about someone's private life, violating the principle Jesus established in Matthew 18:15: "If your brother or sister sins, go and point out their fault, just between the two of you".

Stage 4: The Narrative Building

Various pieces of information begin forming a coherent story: "Tom's been stressed, leaving early, and Ben mentioned he seemed upset during their project meeting. Plus, his wife didn't come to the company picnic. They're probably having marriage problems." The group feels they've solved the mystery of Tom's behavior. But they've actually constructed what Scripture calls "false witness." The ninth commandment specifically addresses this: "You shall not give false testimony against your neighbor" (Exodus 20:16).

Stage 5: The Spreading Network

Once a narrative exists, it spreads beyond the original group. "Did you hear about Tom's marriage problems?" travels from person to person, often losing the uncertainty and speculation that marked its earlier stages. By the third retelling, the theory has transformed into accepted fact. This reflects the warning in Proverbs 26:20: "Without wood a fire goes out; without a gossip a quarrel dies down". Each person who passes along the narrative adds fuel to a fire consuming Tom's reputation.

Stage 6: The Established Truth

In the final stage, the gossip becomes "common knowledge." New employees are warned about Tom's "personal problems." His stress is interpreted through the lens of his supposed marriage troubles.

Tom is now living with the consequences of a narrative that may have no basis in reality. This fulfills the warning in Proverbs 18:21: "The tongue has the power of life and death, and those who love it will eat its fruit".

Breaking the Progression: The Biblical Path Forward

The beauty of understanding this progression is that it can be interrupted at any stage through biblical principles. When you notice yourself moving from observation to speculation, you can choose to follow Jesus's example of going directly to the person with love and concern.

Here are biblical ways to interrupt the progression:

At Stage 1: "Tom seemed stressed today. I should check in with him privately." (Following Galatians 6:2)

At Stage 2: "I'm making assumptions about Tom's situation. Instead of speculating, I'll offer general support." (Following Deuteronomy 19:15)

At Stage 3: "I realize I'm trying to solve a puzzle that isn't mine to solve." (Following Matthew 18:15)

At Stage 4: "We're building a story about Tom without knowing the facts. This violates the principle of not bearing false witness." (Following Exodus 20:16)

At Stage 5: "I shouldn't pass along information about Tom's personal life." (Following Proverbs 26:20)

At Stage 6: "I realize we've been operating on assumptions about Tom. We need to give him the benefit of the doubt." (Following Proverbs 18:21)

Recognizing Gossip's Different Personas

Now that we understand how gossip progresses, let's examine the different personas it adopts to avoid detection.

The Concern Troll: When Care Becomes Character Assassination

The Concern Troll has perfected the art of looking genuinely worried while delivering character assassination with surgical precision. They furrow their brow just right, lower their voice to the perfect tone of concern, and deliver lines like "I'm really worried about Susan's decision-making lately."

What makes them so dangerous is how righteous they sound. They've mastered the caring head tilt and the ability to make you feel like you're witnessing genuine compassion. But here's the tell: their "concern" never leads to actually helping the person they're worried about. Instead, they spread their worry like seeds in fertile soil, recruiting others to share their "concern" and building a case against someone who has no idea she's being discussed.

Concern that bypasses this biblical model and goes straight to community discussion isn't concern—it's gossip wearing a caring mask.

The Prayer Warrior: Too Much Information

Sometimes well-meaning intercessors cross the line from genuine prayer requests into detailed information sharing while maintaining an air of holy concern. They're masters of the spiritual preface: "We really need to pray for Tom and Sharon's marriage—I heard they're sleeping in separate rooms."

Often these sincere believers don't realize how their detailed sharing affects others or crosses privacy boundaries. The heart to pray is genuine, but the approach needs refinement.

Genuine prayer requests focus on general needs: "Please pray for my friend going through a difficult time." But when we can't resist the specifics, we should pause and ask ourselves: Does this prayer request require intimate details to be effective? Does sharing these details honor the person I'm asking prayer for?

James 5:16 encourages us to "pray for each other so that you may be healed", but nowhere does it suggest that effective intercession requires a detailed briefing on someone's private struggles. God already knows the specifics—our role is to pray, not to inform.

The Information Broker: "You Didn't Hear This From Me"

The Information Broker has turned knowing everyone's business into an art form. They pride themselves on being first to know and first to share, often prefacing their broadcasts with "You didn't hear this from me, but..."

They create dependency by positioning themselves as the central hub for community news. But notice what type of information they prioritize: it's rarely good news. This dependency feeds their need to feel valuable and connected, but it comes at the expense of authentic relationships.

The Digital Weapon: Where Screenshots Live Forever

The digital age has given gossip superpowers that previous generations couldn't imagine. Group texts, private message chains, and social media have become virtual echo chambers where character assassination spreads at wifi speed.

These platforms are particularly dangerous because they create an illusion of intimacy and privacy. People say things in group chats they would never say face-to-face, emboldened by the screen barrier. But screenshots live forever, and today's inner circle can become tomorrow's evidence.

The Truth Mixer: Packaging Lies with Facts

The Truth Mixer might be the most sophisticated gossip artist. They've perfected combining accurate information with speculation, opinion, or exaggeration. Because some of what they share is verifiably true, their audience is more likely to swallow the portions that aren't.

"John did miss the important HOA meeting, and I heard it's because he's been having those anger issues again" mixes a factual observation with an unverified claim. This form is particularly insidious because it's harder to refute. When confronted, they can point to the accurate portions and claim they were "just sharing what they knew." But mixing truth with speculation is still gossip—it's just gossip with better packaging.

Building Your Gossip Radar: The Power of Recognition

Developing the ability to recognize these different forms isn't about becoming suspicious of every conversation—it's about gaining the discernment that protects you and others from subtle attacks.

When you can spot gossip in its various disguises, you gain the power to:

- Protect yourself from being drawn into toxic conversations
- Shield others from character assassination

- Redirect conversations toward healthier patterns

- Model integrity in how you speak about absent people

- Create environments where gossip struggles to survive

Responding with Wisdom and Grace

When you spot gossip in action, you don't have to become the conversation police. Often, a simple redirect or gentle boundary is enough to shift the dynamic.

For concern that seems disingenuous: "Have you been able to talk with them directly about this? They might really appreciate knowing you care."

For overly detailed prayer requests: "I can definitely pray for them without needing to know the specifics. God already sees their situation completely."

For information that feels more entertaining than necessary: "I try to focus on my own challenges rather than getting involved in other people's situations."

The goal isn't to shut down every conversation, but to gently steer interactions toward patterns that build up rather than tear down.

The Mirror Moment: Examining Our Own Hearts

We've all played these roles at some point. The key is recognizing when we're slipping into these patterns and choosing a different path forward.

Which character do you recognize in yourself? What underlying need might you be trying to meet through these conversations? Connection? Feeling important? Processing your own hurt? Understanding these motivations helps us find healthier ways to meet those legitimate needs.

These needs are human and understandable. The transformation comes in learning to meet them through life-giving conversations rather than life-draining gossip.

Moving Forward with Discernment

God calls us to be people whose words build up rather than tear down. As we learn to identify gossip's many masks, we become better guardians of our own hearts and protectors of our communities' health.

This discernment doesn't happen overnight, but it grows stronger with practice. Each time you recognize gossip and choose not to participate, you're building the muscle of integrity. Each time you redirect a conversation toward grace, you're creating space for healthier relationships to flourish.

The ability to see clearly what others might miss isn't just protection—it's empowerment. You're no longer at the mercy of conversations that drain your energy and damage your community. You have the tools to recognize, respond, and redirect toward something better.

Now that you can identify gossip in its various disguises, let's explore how to recognize when you're becoming its target—the warning signs that help you prepare and protect yourself before the damage spreads.

Chapter 4: Early Warning Signs: When You're Becoming a Target

After learning to recognize gossip's many disguises, the next crucial skill is recognizing when those masks are being turned toward you. Understanding how gossip operates in general is valuable, but knowing when you're becoming its target can save you from weeks or months of confusion, self-doubt, and unnecessary pain.

Looking back, I realize the signs were there long before I understood what was happening. I dismissed them because I was still new to the company and told myself that people didn't really know me yet. Surely those strange looks, the subtle shifts in energy, and the conversations that seemed to stop when I approached were all in my head. I was being paranoid, overthinking things, reading too much into normal workplace dynamics.

I was wrong. What I initially dismissed as my imagination was actually my intuition warning me that I was becoming the target of a gossip campaign. The challenge of being new to any environment—whether it's a workplace, church, neighborhood, or social group—is that you don't yet know what "normal" looks like. You have no baseline for comparison, no way to differentiate between typical social behaviors and the early signs of coordinated exclusion.

But God gave us instincts for a reason. These early warnings can save us from much deeper pain and give us the power to respond strategically rather than reactively.

These warning signs function like a social smoke detector—designed to alert you before the house catches fire, giving you time to address the problem or protect yourself before the damage spreads.

The Atmosphere Shift: When Your Presence Changes Everything

The first warning sign is often atmospheric—a change in the energy of a room when you enter. This isn't about individual people acting differently; it's about the collective mood shifting in response to your presence, like someone just announced bad news at a celebration.

In healthy environments, your arrival creates neutral or positive energy. People continue their conversations naturally, might smile and nod acknowledgment, or genuinely welcome you into the discussion. Someone might say, "Perfect timing, we were just talking about something you'd find interesting" or "Come join us, we're planning weekend activities." The energy stays consistent or becomes more positive with your presence.

But when gossip is brewing, your presence creates tension that feels intentional and loaded. Conversations don't just pause—they stop with a weight that hangs in the air. The silence isn't natural; it feels calculated, like everyone just got caught discussing something they shouldn't have been.

This atmospheric shift happens because the gossip network unconsciously responds to seeing someone they've been dissecting. They haven't necessarily planned to treat you differently, but the conversation context colors their natural interactions with you. It's like they've been talking about a character in a movie, and suddenly that character walks into the room.

When rooms consistently feel different after you enter them, when your presence seems to suck the oxygen out of casual conversations, something real is happening.

The Information Freeze: Suddenly Living in a News Desert

In healthy environments, information flows naturally, like water finding its way downhill. People share updates about projects, events, or decisions without thinking twice about who needs to know. Someone mentions, "Oh, did you see the email about the schedule change?" and if you missed it, they'll quickly catch you up. When decisions are made that affect you, someone takes the time to loop you in, either formally or through casual conversation.

But when you're becoming a gossip target, information flow around you changes dramatically—you become the person standing in the desert while everyone else enjoys the river.

This often manifests as learning about meetings secondhand, hearing about decisions after they've been implemented, or discovering changes that affect your responsibilities through indirect channels. You might find yourself consistently being the last to know about informal gatherings, group activities, or casual meetups that you would previously have been naturally included in. It's like being quietly uninvited to parties you didn't even know were being planned.

This isn't always malicious initially—sometimes it's unconscious distancing as people become uncomfortable around someone they've been discussing negatively. But when it becomes a pattern, you're witnessing the information freeze in action.

The Alliance Becomes Visible: When Unity Looks Like Opposition

As gossip campaigns develop, the people involved begin showing their unity more openly, like a group of friends who've forgotten they're supposed to include others. What started as subtle coordination becomes increasingly obvious alliance behavior that would make political strategists proud.

This often manifests as certain people consistently supporting each other's ideas in meetings, even when those ideas contradict what they believed last week. They laugh at each other's jokes with enthusiasm usually reserved for professional comedians. They reference conversations and shared experiences that seem designed to highlight their insider status and, by extension, your outsider position.

This visible alliance serves multiple purposes: it reinforces the gossipers' bond with each other, it sends a message to others about which side appears stronger, and it creates psychological pressure on the target by demonstrating their isolation.

Biblical friendship looks different. Proverbs 17:17 tells us "A friend loves at all times, and a brother is born for a time of adversity". True alliances are built on love and support, not opposition to others. When you see alliances that seem primarily defined by who they exclude rather than what they embrace, you're watching artificial unity in action.

The Conversation Redirections: When Your Voice Gets Muted

Pay attention to how conversations change when you try to participate. In healthy environments, people build on what you say, ask follow-up questions, or engage naturally with your contributions. Someone might say, "That's interesting, tell me more about that" or "I hadn't thought of it that way" or even disagree respectfully with something like, "I see your point, but I've had a different experience." Your ideas are received as worthy of consideration, your questions are answered thoughtfully, and your presence adds value to the discussion.

But when gossip is brewing, your contributions often meet the conversational equivalent of a polite but firm security escort.

This often manifests as people acknowledging what you said with a diplomatic "mm-hmm" before immediately steering the conversation elsewhere, like GPS recalculating after taking a wrong turn. Your questions might be answered with minimal enthusiasm before someone quickly changes the subject. Your suggestions might be met with lukewarm responses before the group moves on to more "interesting" topics.

This isn't the same as normal conversational flow where topics naturally evolve. This is deliberate minimization of your voice and influence in group settings, designed to make you feel unheard without anyone having to be overtly rude.

The Empathy Gap: When Understanding Goes Missing

One of the clearest warning signs is when people you previously had normal relationships with suddenly seem to have lost their ability to extend basic human empathy or benefit of the doubt. It's like they've been infected by a virus that specifically targets their compassion receptors.

This often manifests as a complete absence of grace when you make mistakes—just highlighting of errors with laser precision. If you're having a difficult day, there's no understanding—just observation of your mood as evidence of your problematic nature. If you express frustration or concern, there's no validation, just judgment of your attitude as proof that you're exactly as difficult as suspected.

This empathy gap happens because gossip campaigns involve character assassination. Once people accept a negative narrative about you, they interpret everything through that lens, like wearing sunglasses that make everything look dark. Your normal human moments become evidence of character flaws.

Where colleagues once might have said, "She seems stressed, I wonder if everything's okay," they now think, "There she goes being difficult again." The same behavior that would be understood and forgiven in others becomes exhibit A in the case against your character.

Moving Forward with Awareness and Strength

Understanding these warning signs isn't about becoming paranoid or suspicious of every social interaction. It's about developing the discernment to recognize when your environment is becoming unhealthy so you can protect yourself and respond wisely rather than reactively.

Not every awkward moment is a warning sign. Not every social exclusion indicates gossip. But when multiple signs appear together in a consistent pattern, it's time to take them seriously. Trust your instincts, seek wise counsel, and remember that your worth isn't determined by how others choose to treat you.

The goal isn't to become hypervigilant about every social interaction, but to trust the wisdom God gave you through your instincts. Sometimes what feels like paranoia is actually discernment trying to protect you from unnecessary pain.

Recognizing these patterns early gives you power—the power to prepare, to protect your peace, to respond strategically rather than reactively, and to maintain your integrity while navigating difficult dynamics. You're no longer caught off guard by treatment that seems to come from nowhere. Instead, you can see the signs, understand what's happening, and choose your response from a place of strength rather than confusion.

In the next chapter, we'll explore exactly how to use this awareness—how to respond when these warning signs prove accurate, how to navigate the storm strategically, and how to protect your peace while maintaining your integrity when gossip strikes.

Chapter 5: How to Respond When Gossip Strikes

The warning signs you tried to dismiss have proven accurate. The atmosphere shifts, information freezes, and alliances have become undeniably visible. You're no longer wondering if you're being targeted by gossip—you know you are. The question that floods your mind is urgent and desperate: What do I do now?

In those first critical hours and days after realizing you're under attack, every instinct screams for action. You want to defend yourself, set the record straight, confront the people spreading lies, or find some way to regain control of a situation that feels completely out of your hands. The isolation hits like a physical blow, unlike anything you've experienced before.

But here's what I learned during my own crisis: the immediate response often determines whether you'll emerge from this stronger or more wounded. When you're operating from hurt, confusion, and isolation, reactive decisions can actually make the situation worse. Strategic responses, on the other hand, can turn even the most malicious gossip campaign into an opportunity for growth, clarity, and ultimately, vindication.

The goal isn't just survival—it's transformation. Let's explore how to respond in ways that protect your peace, maintain your integrity, and position you for the restoration that's coming.

First Response: Anchor Yourself Before You Act

Your first instinct may be to call friends, family members, or colleagues to explain your side of the story. While support is important, rushing to human defenders before anchoring yourself in truth can lead to decisions you'll later regret.

In healthy environments, when conflicts arise, people often give you the benefit of the doubt and approach you directly with concerns. Colleagues might say, "I heard something that didn't sound like you, can we talk about it?" or "There seems to be some confusion about what happened—can you help me understand your perspective?" But when you're dealing with a gossip campaign, you're operating in a completely different dynamic where people have already chosen sides based on incomplete information.

During my workplace crisis, I learned to literally stop and pray before making any phone calls, sending any emails, or having conversations about what was happening. This wasn't about being super-spiritual—it was about survival. When you're operating from hurt and confusion, you need divine perspective before you need human validation.

Proverbs 3:5-6 became my anchor during this season: "Trust in the Lord with all your heart and lean not on your own understanding; in all your ways submit to him, and he will make your paths straight". When everything around you feels chaotic and confusing, God's wisdom provides the clarity you need to respond strategically rather than reactively.

Jeremiah 1:19 contains a promise that sustained me through the worst days: "They will fight against you but will not overcome you, for I am with you and will rescue you,' declares the Lord". This isn't just comfort—it's strategic truth. The battle you're facing has already been won, but you need to fight from that victory rather than fighting for it.

Resist the Defense Reflex (Even Though Every Cell Wants To)

Every fiber of your being will want to set the record straight immediately. You'll compose mental speeches, draft emails explaining your position, and plan conversations where you can finally share your side of the story. This urgency feels righteous—after all, you're innocent and the truth should be told.

But immediate defense often backfires when dealing with established gossip campaigns. Here's why rushing in can actually make things worse:

You're defending against accusations you may not fully understand. Gossip plays telephone with the truth, so the version you're hearing may be very different from what's actually being said about you.

You're fighting on their chosen battlefield. Gossip thrives on drama and emotional reactions. When you rush to defend yourself, you're playing by their rules—and they've had more practice.

Your emotional state may sabotage your message. When you're hurt, angry, and isolated, you're not operating at peak communication skills. You're more likely to come across as defensive or desperate, which just adds fuel to their narrative.

This doesn't mean never defending yourself—it means doing so strategically rather than reactively. Sometimes the most powerful response is no response at all, allowing your consistent character to speak louder than any words could.

Document Everything: Become a Strategic Observer

Now that you've recognized the patterns, start documenting what you're observing. This serves multiple purposes: it helps you see patterns more clearly, provides concrete information if you need to escalate formally, and gives you something constructive to do with your heightened awareness.

Keep a simple record of incidents:

- Date and time

- Who was involved

- What specifically happened (facts, not interpretations)

- Any witnesses present

- How it affected you

This documentation serves several purposes. It helps you distinguish between isolated incidents and genuine patterns. It provides specific examples if you need to discuss the situation with supervisors or other authorities. And it helps you process your experiences without ruminating endlessly or distorting memories over time.

Seek Wise Counsel Outside the Situation

While you shouldn't rush to defend yourself within the gossip-infected environment, you do need perspective and support. Identify people outside the immediate situation who can offer wisdom, prayer, and objective feedback.

This might include family members who know your character, friends from other areas of your life who can provide reality checks, pastors or spiritual mentors who can offer biblical wisdom, or professional counselors who understand toxic dynamics.

When you share your situation with these trusted advisors, focus on facts rather than feelings initially. Ask them to help you see blind spots, suggest appropriate responses, and pray for wisdom and protection.

These outside perspectives serve as reality checks, helping you distinguish between legitimate concerns about the situation and defensive thinking that isolation might be creating.

Maintain Your Character: The Long Game

This may be the hardest advice to follow, but it's the most important: continue being who you are. Don't change your behavior, lower your standards, or compromise your integrity in response to gossip.

The temptation is strong to become defensive and sharp in all your interactions, withdraw completely from social situations, lower your work standards to avoid standing out, gossip about your gossipers, or try to win people over through desperate people-pleasing.

All of these responses damage your character and give credibility to negative narratives about you. Instead, let your consistent character be your defense. Continue showing up with professionalism, kindness, and integrity. Let your work speak for itself. Treat even your enemies with basic respect—not because they deserve it, but because you do.

This strategy requires immense strength because it feels like you're doing nothing while being attacked. But character consistency is one of the most powerful long-term responses to gossip. It's hard to maintain false narratives about someone whose behavior consistently contradicts those narratives.

During my workplace experience, I made the decision to continue treating everyone with the same respect and professionalism I'd always shown. I didn't always get it right—there were moments when hurt and frustration leaked through, or when I responded more defensively than I intended despite my best efforts. But my overall commitment to maintaining my character remained consistent.

When You're the Witness: Recognizing Gossip About Others

Sometimes you'll find yourself witnessing gossip about someone who isn't present to defend themselves. One particularly common pattern is what I call "the reframer"—someone who takes another person's reasonable approach and reframes it as problematic simply because it's not what they would have done.

Have you ever heard someone retell a situation where you were present and found yourself thinking, "Hold on, that's not how it happened"? Maybe it was just a difference in perspective or approach, but in the retelling, someone gets cast as the villain when there was never a villain to begin with.

The reframer takes someone's reasonable decision—perhaps how they handled a project, managed a situation, or communicated—and reframes it as concerning or wrong because it doesn't match their preferred method. The person being discussed isn't there to explain their reasoning or defend their approach. The reframer isn't interested in understanding different methods; they're upset that someone didn't conform to their expectations.

When you hear this type of criticism about an absent person, you have several options:

Neutral redirect: "I wasn't there, so I can't really comment" or "Different people handle things differently." This protects both the absent person and your own integrity without getting pulled into unfair criticism.

Gentle observation: If you have a relationship with the person and sense they might be open to feedback, you could gently say something like, "I notice we're critiquing someone who isn't here to share their perspective. That doesn't feel fair to them." This approach requires discernment about timing and your relationship with the speaker.

Resist engaging: Whether you choose to redirect or remain silent, avoid the urge to either defend the absent person or pile on with additional criticism. The reframer has already decided the approach was wrong and wants others to agree. Engaging often just feeds the narrative and spreads the criticism further.

Remember that standing up for someone who can't defend themselves often says more about your character than theirs.

Build Strategic Relationships: Your Sanity-Saving Network

While you're being targeted by some, there are likely others in the environment who maintain their integrity and judgment. Identify these people and invest in building genuine relationships with them.

These relationships serve multiple purposes: they provide accurate information about what's really happening, they offer support and encouragement during difficult times, they can serve as character witnesses who know you personally, they help prevent complete isolation within the environment, and they may become allies who can help address the situation constructively.

Don't approach these relationships manipulatively, trying to recruit people to your side. Instead, build genuine connections based on shared values, mutual respect, and common interests. Let people get to know the real you through natural interaction rather than through defensive explanations.

Know When to Address It Directly

While immediate defense is usually unwise, there are times when direct communication becomes necessary. The key is timing, approach, and motivation.

Consider direct conversation when you have a relationship with the person that might allow for honest dialogue, you have specific information about what's being said rather than vague concerns, you can approach the conversation with genuine love rather than defensive anger, and you've prayed about it and sense wisdom to address it.

When you do choose to address gossip directly, follow biblical principles: approach privately first (Matthew 18:15), focus on specific behaviors rather than character attacks, use "I" statements about your experience rather than accusations, seek understanding and reconciliation rather than just vindication, and be prepared for the person to deny, deflect, or become defensive.

Remember that direct confrontation may not resolve the situation and could potentially escalate it. The goal isn't necessarily to convince the other person—it's to faithfully follow biblical principles and maintain your own integrity.

Trust God's Timing for Vindication

The hardest part of responding to gossip attacks is surrendering the timeline to God. You want vindication now. You want people to see the truth immediately. You want the attacks to stop today.

But God's justice operates on His timeline, not ours. Sometimes He vindicates quickly and dramatically. Other times, He allows the process to unfold slowly, using it to refine your character, strengthen your faith, and prepare you for future assignments that require the resilience you're developing now.

Isaiah 54:17 promises, "No weapon forged against you will prevail, and you will refute every tongue that accuses you. This is the heritage of the servants of the Lord, and this is their vindication from me,' declares the Lord". Notice that vindication comes from God, not from your frantic efforts to defend yourself.

This doesn't mean becoming passive or never addressing the situation directly. It means holding your plans and strategies loosely, remaining open to God's guidance, and trusting His heart even when you can't see His hand.

Moving Forward with Strategic Wisdom

Responding to gossip attacks requires both immediate wisdom and long-term perspective. In the crisis moment, anchor yourself in truth, resist reactive responses, and take constructive action through documentation and wise counsel.

For the long term, maintain your character, build strategic relationships, and trust God's timing for vindication. Remember that this battle, while painful, is not pointless. God can use it to strengthen your faith, refine your character, and prepare you for future opportunities that require the resilience you're developing now.

The isolation you feel is real, but it's not permanent. The misunderstanding is painful, but it's not the final word. God sees everything, understands what others cannot, and will ultimately bring justice and restoration in His perfect timing.

Your response to this crisis will shape not just the outcome, but the person you become through it. Choose responses that you'll be proud of when you look back from the place of victory that's coming. The character you build now will serve you for the rest of your life, and the wisdom you gain will help others facing similar battles.

In the next chapter, we'll explore how to find comfort and create safety while these battles are raging—discovering both spiritual strength and practical boundaries that protect your healing without isolating you from the relationships God wants you to experience.

Chapter 6: Suiting Up: Your Daily Armor for Difficult People

Last Thanksgiving, my friend Rebecca called me in a panic. "I need help," she said. "I'm about to walk into three hours with my family, and you know how that goes. My sister will make passive-aggressive comments about my career choices, my uncle will bring up every mistake I made in college, and my mother will somehow make my life decisions all about her. I need more than a good outfit for this— I need divine intervention."

"Sounds like you need to suit up," I told her. "Not with a fancy dress, but with some spiritual armor that actually works."

We've all been there. Whether it's facing a difficult family gathering, walking into a workplace full of tension, or dealing with that neighbor who seems to specialize in drama, some situations require more than just a positive attitude and a prayer. They require what could be called "getting dressed for battle"—except this battle is fought with patience, wisdom, and supernatural peace instead of swords and shields.

Paul understood something about difficult people. In Ephesians 6, he describes spiritual armor not because he was expecting literal warfare, but because he understood that dealing with challenging personalities and toxic environments requires more than human strength. Think of it as getting dressed for the weather, except the forecast calls for a chance of criticism with possible scattered attacks on your character.

The Truth Belt: Your Foundation Garment

The belt of truth functions like a good pair of supportive undergarments—not glamorous, but absolutely essential for everything else to work properly. This involves knowing who you are before anyone else tries to tell you who you should be.

"Stand firm then, with the belt of truth buckled around your waist" (Ephesians 6:14). *"You will know the truth, and the truth will set you free"* (John 8:32).

Rebecca's sister had a particular talent for making observations like, "Well, I suppose not everyone can be successful in traditional ways," while looking directly at Rebecca's freelance graphic design career. Without the truth belt, Rebecca would spend the entire dinner defending her life choices or spiraling into self-doubt about whether she'd made the right decisions.

But with the truth belt securely fastened, Rebecca could think, "I know who I am. I'm talented, I love my work, I pay my bills, and I help people bring their creative visions to life." Her sister's comments became like rain hitting a good raincoat—they rolled right off instead of soaking through to cause damage.

The truth belt isn't about convincing yourself everything is perfect. It's about anchoring yourself in facts rather than other people's opinions. I am loved by God. I am doing my best with what I know. I am growing and learning. I am not defined by my worst moments or other people's worst interpretations of my actions.

The process sometimes feels like a superhero getting ready for action, except instead of fighting crime, you're preparing to not take your mother-in-law's cooking critiques personally.

The Breastplate of Righteousness: Heart Protection

The breastplate protects your heart from the arrows of criticism, guilt, and condemnation that people love to shoot your way. Think of it as emotional body armor that deflects other people's attempts to make you feel bad about yourself.

"With the breastplate of righteousness in place" (Ephesians 6:14). "He will cover you with his feathers, and under his wings you will find refuge; his faithfulness will be your shield and rampart" (Psalm 91:4).

Rebecca struggled with her family's tendency to criticize her life choices, but the breastplate reminded her that God's acceptance of her wasn't dependent on their approval. When her uncle made his usual comments about her "unconventional" lifestyle, the breastplate helped her remember that she was righteous in God's eyes—not because of her perfect behavior, but because of His perfect love.

The breastplate doesn't make you arrogant or defensive. It just reminds your heart that you don't have to internalize every criticism or carry guilt for not meeting everyone's expectations. You're already accepted by the One whose opinion matters most.

Picture this as wearing really good emotional protection for any strenuous activity involving difficult people—supportive, practical, and absolutely necessary for maintaining your peace.

The Peace Shoes: Keeping Your Footing

The shoes of peace function like having really good traction on slippery ground. When everyone around you is slipping into drama, criticism, or chaos, you stay steady on your feet.

"And with your feet fitted with the readiness that comes from the gospel of peace" (Ephesians 6:15). *"Peace I leave with you; my peace I give you. I do not give to you as the world gives. Do not let your hearts be troubled and do not be afraid"* (John 14:27).

During Rebecca's Thanksgiving preparation, she mentioned how her family gatherings often felt like walking on ice—one wrong step and everyone would be sliding into old arguments and hurt feelings. The peace shoes would help her stay balanced and calm regardless of how slippery the conversation became.

"Think of it this way," I told her. "You can't control whether your uncle brings up your college drinking stories again, but you can control whether you slip into defensiveness or stay grounded in peace."

Peace doesn't mean being passive or letting people walk all over you. It means having inner stability that doesn't depend on external circumstances. It's the difference between being a leaf blown around by every emotional storm and being a tree that bends but doesn't break.

The Faith Shield: Deflecting the Unexpected

The shield of faith functions like having really good reflexes for blocking sudden attacks. You know those moments when someone says something completely unexpected and hurtful? The shield deflects those arrows before they can penetrate your heart.

"In addition to all this, take up the shield of faith, with which you can extinguish all the flaming arrows of the evil one" (Ephesians 6:16). "The Lord your God is with you, the Mighty Warrior who saves. He will take great delight in you; in his love he will no longer rebuke you, but will rejoice over you with singing" (Zephaniah 3:17).

Rebecca discovered this when her sister made an unexpected comment about Rebecca "never finishing anything she starts." The comment came out of nowhere and stung, but instead of letting it wound her, the shield of faith helped her think, "That says more about her need to feel superior than about my character or accomplishments."

Faith doesn't mean pretending attacks don't hurt. It means trusting that God sees the whole picture, knows your heart, and will ultimately bring justice and vindication in His timing. The shield deflects the arrows so you can keep moving forward without getting stuck nursing wounds.

This feels like having really good emotional reflexes—when someone throws criticism your way, you automatically deflect it instead of catching it and carrying it around all day.

The Salvation Helmet: Protecting Your Thoughts

The helmet protects your mind from the toxic thoughts that difficult people love to plant. You know that voice that starts whispering, "Maybe they're right. Maybe you are too sensitive. Maybe you really are the problem."

"Take the helmet of salvation" (Ephesians 6:17). "You keep him in perfect peace whose mind is stayed on you, because he trusts in you" (Isaiah 26:3).

The helmet reminds your brain whose voice you're really hearing and whose opinions actually matter. When Rebecca's mother started her usual guilt trip about Rebecca not visiting enough, the helmet protected her thoughts from spiraling into false guilt and self-condemnation.

"I started thinking of it as a protective shield that reminded me God delights in me," Rebecca said. "When my brain wanted to spiral into self-doubt, I could remember that God's voice is the one that matters most."

The Word Sword: Your Offensive Tool

The sword of the Spirit is God's Word, and it's the only offensive weapon in this spiritual wardrobe. But instead of attacking people, you use it to cut through lies, confusion, and deception.

"And take the helmet of salvation and the sword of the Spirit, which is the word of God" (Ephesians 6:17). "For the word of God is alive and active. Sharper than any double-edged sword, it penetrates even to dividing soul and spirit, joints and marrow; it judges the thoughts and attitudes of the heart" (Hebrews 4:12).

When someone tries to tell you who you are, you respond with what God says about you. When circumstances try to convince you that the situation is hopeless, you remember God's promises. When your emotions try to take you on a roller coaster ride, you speak truth to your own heart.

Rebecca used this when her sister made her usual comments about her career choices. Instead of arguing or getting defensive, she quietly reminded herself of specific truths: "I am fearfully and wonderfully made" (Psalm 139:14). When her mother started guilt-tripping about visits, Rebecca silently repeated, "God has not given me a spirit of fear, but of power, love, and sound mind" (2 Timothy 1:7). The conversations moved on, but Rebecca's peace remained intact.

Putting On Your Armor: A Daily Practice

The beautiful thing about this spiritual armor is that it becomes a daily practice that transforms how you approach every interaction. Like getting dressed each morning, putting on your armor can become a routine that prepares you for whatever the day might bring.

It's important to understand that spiritual armor is preparation, not a magic shield that makes difficult people suddenly become easy to handle. You may still feel the sting of harsh words or the exhaustion that comes from navigating toxic dynamics. The armor doesn't eliminate these challenges—it helps you face them from a position of spiritual strength rather than emotional vulnerability.

Morning Armor Routine:

Ground yourself in prayer first, asking God to clothe you with His armor before facing the day ahead of you.

1. **Truth Belt:** Remind yourself of who you are in God's eyes before anyone else gets to speak into your day

2. **Righteousness Breastplate:** Acknowledge your acceptance by God and let that protect your heart from criticism

3. **Peace Shoes:** Choose to walk in peace regardless of others' emotional states

4. **Faith Shield:** Prepare to deflect unexpected attacks with trust in God's goodness

5. **Salvation Helmet:** Guard your thoughts against lies and toxic thinking patterns

6. **Word Sword:** Arm yourself with specific scriptures that speak truth to your situation

Then step forward, knowing you're equipped for whatever comes.

Rebecca spent a few minutes in her car, praying what was on her heart before going into her parents' house. The gathering wasn't perfect—her sister still made passive-aggressive comments, her uncle still brought up old stories, and her mother still tried to center herself in every conversation. Rebecca felt the familiar stabs of frustration and hurt, but she handled them differently.

When her sister made the usual comments, Rebecca stayed peaceful instead of getting defensive. When her uncle brought up old stories, she responded with gentle humor rather than shame. When her mother tried to make everything about herself, Rebecca listened without taking responsibility for her mother's emotions.

"It wasn't that the armor made everything easy," Rebecca said later. "I was still exhausted afterward—dealing with difficult people is just draining. But it was the first family gathering in years where I didn't go home feeling beaten up and questioning myself. I felt tired but not defeated."

Your Daily Wardrobe Decision

Tomorrow morning, before you get dressed for whatever challenges await, take a moment to put on your spiritual armor. It doesn't require a dramatic prayer or lengthy ritual, just a simple acknowledgment that you're choosing to face the day equipped with more than your own strength.

Think of it as choosing the right outfit for the weather. If it's going to be emotionally stormy, you need good protection. If you're walking into a situation with difficult people, you need appropriate gear. If you're facing criticism or conflict, you need armor that actually works.

The goal isn't to become defensive or expect the worst from everyone. It's to be prepared for whatever comes your way, equipped with peace that doesn't depend on other people's moods, identity that doesn't waver based on criticism, and strength that comes from knowing you're loved and protected by the Creator of the universe.

Some days you'll need the full armor. Other days, just the truth belt and peace shoes will do. But every day, you have the choice to face life's challenges equipped with spiritual resources that actually work.

Remember that putting on spiritual armor doesn't eliminate the physical and emotional toll that difficult people can take on you. Even with the best preparation, you may still feel drained after challenging encounters. This is normal and doesn't mean you're doing anything wrong. Spiritual armor helps you maintain your integrity and peace during difficult interactions, but it doesn't make you superhuman. Plan for rest and recovery after particularly challenging situations—this is wisdom, not weakness.

Learning to put on this armor daily creates a foundation of strength that serves you whether you're facing outright gossip attacks or simply navigating the everyday challenges of difficult relationships. But even with the best spiritual preparation, there are times when the attacks feel overwhelming and you need something more than armor—you need a place of refuge where you can rest and find comfort in what's truly unchanging.

Sometimes the battle is so intense or prolonged that you need to step away from active resistance and simply find shelter in God's presence. That's where we're headed next: discovering how to create safe spaces of comfort in God's truth, places where you can retreat to be reminded of who you really are when the world's voices grow too loud, and boundaries that protect not just your peace but your very soul.

Chapter 7: Finding Comfort in God's Truth While Creating Safe Spaces

After Rebecca's successful Thanksgiving dinner—the one where she "suited up" with spiritual armor and actually enjoyed herself—she called me with an unexpected question. "I'm glad I survived the day," she said, "but now what? I can't live in full armor mode forever. I need to figure out how to actually heal from all the family drama, not just protect myself from it."

Rebecca had discovered what many people learn after surviving difficult seasons: protection is essential, but it's not the same as healing. You can develop all the coping strategies in the world, but at some point, your soul needs more than just defense mechanisms. It needs sanctuary, comfort, and genuine safety to process what you've been through and rebuild what was damaged.

There comes a point in every battle when the sword feels too heavy to carry—not because you've given up, but because your spirit is begging for rest. You've prayed, you've cried, you've done your best to stay composed while the world whispers lies behind your back.

Though you've remained standing, your knees are beginning to buckle under the invisible weight of it all.

This chapter is for that moment—when you need to fall into the arms of the One who never lets go, while also learning to create some practical breathing room where healing can actually happen.

When Your Soul Needs a Sanctuary

Rebecca discovered this during the weeks following that Thanksgiving dinner. She'd gotten good at putting on her spiritual armor each morning and maintaining her composure during family interactions. But by evening, she was emotionally exhausted from the constant vigilance required to navigate those challenging relationships.

"I felt like I was running on fumes," she told me. "I could handle the daily interactions, but I was forgetting what peace actually felt like. I needed more than just survival strategies—I needed to remember who I was when I wasn't defending myself."

Have you ever tried convincing yourself you're over something, repeating positive affirmations about being "blessed and highly favored," but then a random memory or familiar voice brings you right back to that emotional storm? That's not weakness—that's your soul signaling that it needs more than just positive thinking. It needs genuine comfort and time to heal.

"The Lord is close to the brokenhearted and saves those who are crushed in spirit" (Psalm 34:18). "Come to me, all you who are weary and burdened, and I will give you rest" (Matthew 11:28).

In healthy environments, when you're hurting, people naturally give you space to process. They don't push for details you're not ready to share or take your need for quiet personally. They understand that some wounds need time and tenderness to mend properly.

But when you're dealing with gossip situations, that natural space often doesn't exist. People want information. They want to know your side. They want to help by sharing what they've heard. The very people you need space from keep showing up in your emotional recovery room, like well-meaning visitors who don't realize the patient needs rest more than conversation.

Emotional Safety With Your Creator

Here's what I've learned about finding comfort in God's truth: with Him, you don't need a mask. You don't have to hurry your healing or have it all together to spend time with Him. He doesn't gaslight, guilt-trip, or rush. He listens. He waits. He sees straight through the "I'm fine" and says, "I know you're not, and that's okay. Tell me anyway."

When David was running from King Saul, hiding in caves and constantly looking over his shoulder, he wrote some of his most beautiful psalms about God's protection and comfort. Psalm 31:19-

20 says, "How abundant are the good things that you have stored up for those who fear you... In the shelter of your presence you hide them from all human intrigues; in your dwelling you keep them safe from accusing tongues".

David understood something profound: there's a difference between the protection God provides in the midst of battle and the comfort He offers in the secret place of His presence. Both are necessary, but they serve different purposes.

Remember Elijah under the broom tree (1 Kings 19:4-8). This bold prophet was running for his life, exhausted and overwhelmed. He found a spot under a tree and told God, "I've had enough." Instead of scolding him for his lack of faith, God provided food and rest, then spoke to him—not in dramatic fire or earthquake, but in a gentle whisper.

God meets you in your exhaustion, not your performance. He tends to you like a gardener with delicate hands—healing you without forcing, listening without interrupting, loving you even when you feel unlovable.

There's something freeing about knowing you're not too much for God—not too emotional, not too broken, not too slow to heal. You're just loved.

Creating Boundaries That Heal Instead of Hide

While you're finding comfort in God's presence, you also need some practical protection from the chaos around you. The goal isn't to build walls that keep you isolated forever, but to create healthy boundaries that give you space to heal while keeping you available for the genuine relationships God wants you to experience.

Think of boundaries like the walls of a healing garden, they're not meant to keep you locked in, but to create a safe space where new growth can actually happen. A garden wall keeps out rabbits that would eat the young plants, but it has gates for friends who want to enjoy the beauty you're cultivating.

Rebecca learned this distinction as she continued processing her family dynamics beyond that successful Thanksgiving dinner. While putting on spiritual armor had helped her survive the day, she realized she needed ongoing protection to heal from years of accumulated hurt from her sister's critical comments.

"My first instinct was to avoid all family gatherings forever," Rebecca said. "But that would have meant missing out on relationships with nieces, nephews, and other family members I genuinely enjoyed. I needed to figure out how to stay connected to the good relationships while protecting myself from the toxic ones."

Instead of building walls against everyone, Rebecca learned to create what she called "smart boundaries"—protection that was selective rather than universal. She stopped engaging with her sister's critical comments but continued enjoying conversations with cousins who were genuinely supportive. She declined to attend small family gatherings where tension was predictable but still participated in larger celebrations where the dynamics were more diffused and manageable.

The Three-Circle Approach: Organizing Your Relationships for Healing

During my own difficult season, I developed what became known as the "three-circle strategy" for managing relationships when you're vulnerable and healing. Instead of treating everyone the same or shutting everyone out, this approach recognizes that different people deserve different levels of access to your heart during sensitive times.

Inner Circle: Your Safe Harbor These are the people who get full access—your spouse, closest friend, or spiritual mentor. They've proven they're safe with your heart, they can handle the messy details without trying to fix everything, and they love you enough to tell you the truth even when it's hard to hear.

For Rebecca, this was her sister Amy (not the critical one from Thanksgiving—families are complicated) and her longtime mentor from church. "These were the people who could handle me crying about the same situation for the third time without making me feel weak or dramatic," Rebecca said.

Middle Circle: Your Supportive Network These are people who care about you and can offer encouragement, but don't need to know every detail of what you're going through. They get the general idea without the full emotional download. This might include work friends, church members, neighbors you trust, or family members who are supportive but not necessarily your closest confidants.

With these people, you might say something like, "I'm working through some challenging family dynamics, but I'm handling it well. Thanks for asking."

Outer Circle: Everyone Else This includes acquaintances, colleagues you don't know well, and anyone who hasn't earned the right to your vulnerable moments. They get surface-level interaction only—polite, professional, but not personal.

This isn't about being cold or unfriendly. It's about wisdom. Some people haven't demonstrated they can handle your heart with care, and during healing seasons, you can't afford to find out the hard way.

"Do not give dogs what is sacred; do not throw your pearls to pigs. If you do, they may trample them under their feet, and turn and tear you to pieces" (Matthew 7:6).

The Art of Graceful Redirection

You'll need some go-to responses for people who ask for more than you're ready to share. The key is to redirect rather than explain why you won't share, which just creates more curiosity and potential drama.

When someone asks probing questions about your situation: "I appreciate your concern. I'm handling it appropriately and focusing on moving forward."

When someone wants to share gossip they've heard about you: "I'd rather not get into all that. How are things going with your family?"

When someone offers unsolicited advice: "Thanks for caring. I've got some good support helping me work through this."

Rebecca discovered the power of these simple redirections during family interactions following that pivotal Thanksgiving. "I used to feel obligated to explain everything to anyone who asked," she said. "But I learned that most people don't actually need the details, they just need to know I'm okay and handling things well."

When Boundaries Feel Exhausting

Maintaining protection requires energy, and you may experience what I call "boundary fatigue"—feeling drained from constantly monitoring interactions, dreading previously enjoyable activities, or becoming overly suspicious of everyone's motives.

This is normal and temporary. Here's what helps:

Schedule downtime with completely safe people where you can drop your guard entirely. These are relationships where you don't have to weigh every word or wonder about hidden agendas.

Spend time alone in activities that restore your energy. Sometimes the best boundary is simply being by yourself where no one can ask questions, offer advice, or require emotional energy from you.

Remember your purpose. Remind yourself why you're in particular environments and what God wants you to accomplish there. This keeps you focused on your mission rather than getting lost in relationship management.

Rebecca found this helpful during extended family events. "I reminded myself that I was there to maintain relationships with people I genuinely loved, not to win approval from everyone," she said. "That helped me stay engaged where it mattered while protecting myself from unnecessary drama."

Creating Restoration Rituals

During healing seasons, you need activities that remind you who you are outside of the conflict or drama. These "restoration rituals" become anchors that keep you connected to your true identity when other people are trying to redefine you.

For Rebecca, this meant returning to painting, something she'd abandoned years earlier during busy work seasons. "Every weekend, I'd set up my easel and lose myself in creating something beautiful," she said. "Those paintings reminded me that I could create beauty and find joy, even when my family relationships felt complicated."

These activities serve multiple purposes: they give you a break from processing difficult emotions, they remind you of your strengths and gifts, they connect you with people who see the best in you, and they create positive experiences that balance the negative ones you're working through.

"He has made everything beautiful in its time" (Ecclesiastes 3:11).

Prayer as Your Daily Refuge

When you're hurt by betrayal or weighed down by gossip, prayer becomes more than just asking God to fix everything. It's your daily connection with the One who sees the whole picture, knows your heart completely, and loves you unconditionally.

A prayer for this season might be: "Lord, I come to You with a heavy heart. I've been hurt, and I feel betrayed. But I choose to trust in Your healing power. Please give me wisdom about who to trust and how to protect the heart You've given me. Help me create space for healing while staying open to the relationships You want me to have. Give me peace that passes understanding and strength for each day. Heal my wounds, restore my spirit, and help me forgive. In Jesus' name, Amen."

When People Don't Like Your Boundaries

Some people will take your boundaries personally. They'll say you're being "difficult" or "not the same person you used to be." This is especially hard when it comes from people you care about.

In healthy relationships, when you explain that you need some space to heal, people respond with understanding: "Of course, take all the time you need. I'm here when you're ready." They might not fully understand what you're going through, but they respect your need for protection.

In unhealthy dynamics, people often react to boundaries as personal rejection. They may push harder, guilt you for having limits, or interpret your self-protection as evidence that you really are the problem.

Here's the truth: people who respect your boundaries are revealing their character. People who fight against your boundaries are also revealing their character. Both responses give you valuable information about who is safe and who isn't.

The Gradual Opening

Boundaries aren't meant to be permanent walls. As you heal and grow stronger, you can gradually assess whether it's safe to open up certain relationships again. But this should happen slowly and intentionally, not because people pressure you or make you feel guilty.

You'll know you're ready to consider relaxing some boundaries when you can think about the original situation without intense emotional charge, you feel strong in your identity and purpose, you're no longer easily shaken by criticism, and you have clarity about what kind of relationship you want with specific people going forward.

Rebecca found this process took about eight months. "I started testing the waters with a few family members who had shown genuine change in how they communicated," she said. "Some relationships did get restored to an even healthier place than before. Others remained at a more distant but peaceful level. But I got to choose based on wisdom rather than just hope or obligation."

By the end of that year, Rebecca had developed skills she carried into every relationship—not just family dynamics, but workplace interactions, friendships, and community involvement. She learned to recognize when someone was safe with her heart and when protection was needed. Most importantly, she discovered that healing was possible without requiring anyone else to change first.

"The best part," Rebecca told me in our final conversation about this season, "is that I'm no longer afraid of difficult people or situations. I know how to protect myself while staying loving. I know how to find God's comfort when people disappoint me. And I know that peace is something I can create regardless of what's happening around me."

Moving Forward with Both Comfort and Protection

Finding comfort in God's truth while creating practical safe spaces isn't contradictory—it's wisdom. You can rest in His love while also being smart about who gets access to your vulnerable moments. You can trust God's protection while also taking practical steps to guard your peace.

The goal is developing the confidence to engage authentically while protecting what matters most. As you practice these skills—both the spiritual discipline of finding comfort in God and the practical wisdom of healthy boundaries—you'll discover that peace is possible even when external chaos continues.

Your healing doesn't depend on other people changing their behavior or apologizing for their treatment of you. It depends on your willingness to receive God's comfort and create the conditions where that healing can take root and flourish.

In the next chapter, we'll explore how to find peace amongst the chaos—discovering that true peace isn't dependent on perfect circumstances or other people's behavior, but can be cultivated even in the midst of ongoing challenges and difficult relationships.

Chapter 8: Finding Peace Amongst the Chaos

You can learn to protect yourself from gossip attacks. You can master the art of boundaries and develop strategies for responding wisely to difficult people. But eventually, you realize something profound: external strategies are essential, but they're not enough. You can document every incident, set perfect boundaries, and master every response technique, but if your internal world remains chaotic, you're still at the mercy of other people's actions and opinions.

There comes a point when protection mode feels exhausting, when you realize you want more than just survival—you want genuine peace that doesn't depend on managing everyone else's behavior. The question becomes: Is that even possible?

The world is loud. It pulls you in every direction, telling you what to think, how to act, and who you should be. Every conversation, every notification, every sideways glance adds to the cacophony of expectations, comparisons, and judgment. But here's what the journey through gossip attacks teaches you: the real issue isn't the external chaos—it's that we've forgotten how to create internal quiet.

When you're under attack, you can feel like you're carrying around a radio that's stuck between stations, picking up static and distorted voices no matter where you go. The noise isn't just external anymore; it has moved inside your head and taken up permanent residence.

Understanding What We're Really Silencing

The most dangerous noise isn't always the loudest. It's the whispers overheard in bathrooms about your "attitude problem." It's the deliberate way conversations stop when you appear. It's the group messages you discover where people are building cases against your character or performance.

This noise gets into your head and starts playing like a soundtrack of self-doubt on endless repeat. Unlike healthy environments where conflicts get addressed directly and people assume good intentions, toxic environments create constant, intentional noise designed to make you question everything about yourself.

The experience can make every comment feel loaded with hidden meaning, every social interaction become a minefield of potential criticism. You start editing who you are, walking on eggshells, changing your natural personality to avoid becoming the center of negative attention again. Before you know it, you're carrying around a backpack full of other people's opinions and assumptions, and it's breaking your spirit.

Gossip wears a mask, pretending to be harmless sharing or legitimate concern. But underneath, it's corrosive. It doesn't just make you feel alone; it tries to convince you that you're not worth defending, that maybe you really are the problem everyone seems to think you are.

John 8:44 identifies the devil as the father of lies, and gossip becomes his favorite playground. He wants you to question your worth through carefully crafted deception designed to throw you off course. But here's the freeing truth: you don't have to keep listening. Not every voice deserves a seat at your table—some voices don't even deserve to be heard through the window.

Practical Steps to Reclaim Your Internal Quiet

Turn Down the Volume (You Control the Remote)

You have more control than you think over which voices get airtime in your mind. When you realize you're spending more mental energy processing what critics might be thinking than focusing on your actual purpose and calling, it's time to reclaim control of your mental space.

Think of your peace like your phone's battery—if you let every app run in the background, it drains fast. You don't need to accept every invitation to drama, respond to every criticism, or analyze every interaction for hidden meaning.

1 Peter 5:10: "And the God of all grace, who called you to his eternal glory in Christ, after you have suffered a little while, will himself restore you and make you strong, firm and steadfast".

You can create "volume controls" for your mental space. Important voices—God, people who genuinely love you, trusted mentors—get full volume. Casual acquaintances get moderate volume. Critics and gossips get muted or turned off entirely.

Consider the mental weight you're giving to various opinions. Are you treating a casual acquaintance's criticism with the same gravity as feedback from someone who knows and loves you deeply? That imbalance drains your peace and distorts your perspective.

Replace Lies With Truth (Your Daily Reprogramming)

When negative thoughts flood your mind like a broken dam, you need truth ready to speak back. This isn't just positive thinking, it's spiritual warfare fought with scripture rather than emotions.

When thoughts like "Maybe I am the problem" start spiraling, immediately counter with God's truth: "I am God's handiwork, created for good works" (Ephesians 2:10). When criticism makes you question your worth, remember: "I can do all things through Christ who strengthens me" (Philippians 4:13).

This practice requires intentionality. Write truth where you'll see it throughout the day—on your bathroom mirror, in your car, on your computer screen. When the lies get loud, you'll have truth ready to speak back.

"We demolish arguments and every pretension that sets itself up against the knowledge of God, and we take captive every thought to make it obedient to Christ" (2 Corinthians 10:5).

Use Prayer as Your Anchor in the Storm

When everything feels chaotic and the noise becomes overwhelming, prayer becomes your anchor. It doesn't have to be fancy or rehearsed—just honest. Even a quiet "Lord, help me hear Your voice above all others" can shift everything.

Prayer isn't just asking God to fix your circumstances; it's aligning your heart with His perspective. Psalm 46:10 says, "Be still, and know that I am God". Sometimes the most powerful prayer is simply getting quiet enough to remember who's really in control.

"Do not be anxious about anything, but in every situation, by prayer and petition, with thanksgiving, present your requests to God. And the peace of God, which transcends all understanding, will guard your hearts and your minds in Christ Jesus" (Philippians 4:6-7).

Develop "centering prayers" that you can use before entering potentially difficult situations: "God, help me respond from peace instead of reacting from hurt." These simple prayers become anchors that keep you grounded in truth rather than tossed about by emotions.

Create Quiet Zones in Your Life

Peace requires intentional cultivation. You need spaces and times that are consistently quiet, where the world's noise can't penetrate and your spirit can remember what stillness feels like.

This might be early morning time before anyone else wakes up—no phone, no news, no processing yesterday's conflicts. Just you and God, remembering who you were before the world started telling you who you should be.

Maybe it's evening time without podcasts or music, allowing yourself to experience silence and actually hear your own thoughts instead of just reactions to everyone else's opinions.

These quiet zones aren't escapes from reality—they're investments in your ability to handle reality with grace and wisdom.

"In quietness and trust is your strength" (Isaiah 30:15).

Living From Unshakeable Security

Peace isn't about having perfect circumstances—it's about staying anchored to truth when everything around you is loud and chaotic. When you've been through gossip attacks, you discover whether your foundation is built on rock or sand.

In supportive relationships, your security comes naturally through affirmation and positive feedback. But when those external supports are removed or turned against you, you discover what you're really standing on. This painful revelation becomes a gift: it forces you to find unshakeable security in God rather than in human approval.

"Therefore everyone who hears these words of mine and puts them into practice is like a wise man who built his house on the rock" (Matthew 7:24).

When you anchor yourself deeply in God's love and truth, other people's opinions become just that—opinions. They can't define you anymore because you know whose voice really matters.

The goal isn't to live somewhere you never hear criticism—that place doesn't exist. The goal is to live so deeply rooted in who you truly are that external noise can't shake your foundation.

You don't have to defend yourself when you're walking in truth. Letting go of the need to control how others perceive you isn't giving up—it's giving it over to the One who sees every hidden motive and hears every silent prayer.

The Transformation That Changes Everything

When you stop participating in the noise, something remarkable happens. You demonstrate that there's another way to live—that you don't have to be controlled by other people's opinions, drama, or dysfunction.

People notice when you stop reacting to every provocation, when you maintain your peace despite the chaos around you, when you treat others with kindness even when they don't deserve it. Your peace becomes a testimony to God's power and an invitation for others to find the same security you've discovered.

This isn't about becoming passive or letting people walk all over you. It's about responding from strength rather than reacting from woundedness. It's about choosing your battles wisely and fighting them from a place of inner security rather than desperate self-defense.

"But the fruit of the Spirit is love, joy, peace, forbearance, kindness, goodness, faithfulness, gentleness and self-control. Against such things there is no law" (Galatians 5:22-23).

The peace you've fought for and won becomes a gift you can offer to others who are still struggling with chaos. You become living proof that it's possible to maintain your integrity, protect your heart, and find genuine peace even in the most difficult circumstances.

From Internal Peace to External Influence

This transformation from someone who was controlled by external noise to someone who has found unshakeable internal peace isn't the end of your story—it's preparation for the next chapter. The resilience you've built, the boundaries you've learned to create, and the peace you've discovered position you to become the kind of person who can influence environments positively.

Your journey from victim to survivor to someone who has found genuine peace offers hope to others who are still in the midst of the storm. The quiet strength you've developed becomes the foundation for building healthy relationships, supporting others through their battles, and creating cultures of truth rather than speculation.

The chaos you've learned to navigate with peace becomes the training ground for helping others find their way through similar storms. Your hard-won wisdom about maintaining inner quiet in the midst of external noise becomes a beacon for others who are still learning to distinguish between the voices that matter and the ones that don't.

2 Corinthians 1:3-4: "Praise be to the God and Father of our Lord Jesus Christ, the Father of compassion and the God of all comfort, who comforts us in all our troubles, so that we can comfort those in any trouble with the comfort we ourselves receive from God".

The peace you've found isn't just for you—it's meant to overflow into every relationship and environment you influence. When you've learned to live from unshakeable security, you become someone who can help create the kind of communities where gossip struggles to survive and healthy communication thrives.

In the next chapter, we'll explore how to put this internal transformation into external action—building gossip-free environments through intentional leadership, whether you're currently in authority or preparing for future opportunities to shape the culture around you.

Chapter 9: Building Gossip-Free Environments: Leadership in Action

The peace you've cultivated in the midst of chaos wasn't meant to end with you. The internal transformation you've experienced—learning to silence destructive voices, anchoring yourself in truth, and finding unshakeable security in God—positions you to become an agent of change in every environment you enter.

Whether you hold an official leadership title or not, you have the power to shape the culture around you. Every person in any organization—from entry-level to executive—either contributes to a healthy environment or enables a toxic one. The question isn't whether you have influence; it's what kind of influence you'll choose to exercise.

Leadership is not just a privilege—it's a profound responsibility. When you accept the role of guiding others, you become accountable not only for results but for the culture you create. Every decision, every response, and every conversation either builds trust or erodes it. The weight of that responsibility becomes especially clear when dealing with gossip and toxic communication.

"From everyone who has been given much, much will be demanded; and from the one who has been entrusted with much, much more will be asked" (Luke 12:48).

The Hidden Cost of Toxic Culture

In healthy leadership environments, people bring their best ideas forward without fear. Meetings are collaborative spaces where different perspectives are welcomed. Team members approach each other directly when conflicts arise, knowing that honest conversation leads to resolution rather than retaliation. There's a predictable rhythm to how things work—clear expectations, consistent responses, and reliable support.

But in gossip-infected environments, everything changes. There's no norm, and nearly everything seems suspect. The same behavior that was praised last week might be criticized today, depending on who's in favor and who's not. People spend mental energy trying to decode hidden meanings in casual comments, wondering if that slightly cooler "good morning" means they're in trouble or if they're reading too much into things.

When team members start second-guessing each other and living in fear of becoming the subject of office speculation, productivity suffers. Innovation—that bold force that needs trust and openness—quietly steps aside. People stop feeling like a team and start feeling like they're navigating a minefield alone.

"A house divided against itself cannot stand" (Matthew 12:25, NIV).

The hard truth is that sometimes the whispers start at the top. When those in leadership positions add fuel to gossip through casual comments, show favoritism, or allow harmful chatter to circulate unaddressed, they're actively contributing to a broken culture.

This is the cost of passive leadership. Your words carry weight. What you model becomes the standard others follow. The environments you tolerate are the environments you're creating.

Zero Tolerance, 100% Respect

Creating a gossip-free environment isn't about becoming the conversation police or imposing rigid rules that make people afraid to speak. It's about establishing a culture where respect is the default and direct communication is the norm.

"Therefore encourage one another and build each other up, just as in fact you are doing" (1 Thessalonians 5:11).

The healthiest organizations create what could be called "psychological safety with accountability." People feel safe to share ideas, admit mistakes, and express concerns—but they're also held to a standard of treating others with dignity and addressing conflicts constructively.

When leaders refuse to entertain gossip, others take note. The simple redirect of "Have you talked to them directly about this? I'd encourage you to start there" sends a clear message about expectations without creating shame or defensiveness.

Regular one-on-one conversations become opportunities for people to share concerns before they turn into whispered complaints. When leaders hear about conflicts secondhand, bringing the involved parties together for honest conversation works better than allowing speculation to fill the void.

Building Prevention Systems

Prevention beats correction every time. Creating systems that naturally discourage gossip while encouraging healthy communication makes the difference between reactive management and proactive leadership.

Transparency as a Foundation: When people understand what's happening and why decisions are made, they're less likely to fill gaps with speculation. Clear communication channels give people appropriate outlets for their concerns rather than forcing them into hallway conversations.

When you're new to leadership and inheriting a gossip culture: Start by observing patterns without making immediate judgments. Resist the pressure to "fix things quickly" by taking disciplinary action based on surface-level information or whoever speaks up first. What appears to be gossip may actually be people trying to report legitimate concerns or cope with poor communication systems and unaddressed problems.

Focus on building individual relationships and trust before attempting major cultural shifts. These relationships create the foundation for people to bring issues directly to you rather than discussing them with colleagues. Set clear expectations for your direct reports while being patient with broader organizational change.

Document concerning patterns and address them systematically rather than reactively. Look for whether you're dealing with a few problematic individuals or systemic communication breakdowns that require different solutions entirely. Sometimes the real issue isn't the people talking, but the lack of proper channels for addressing legitimate workplace concerns.

Remember that changing established culture takes time—measure progress in months, not weeks. Taking this patient, systematic approach prevents good people from getting unfairly targeted and helps you understand the real dynamics before making changes that could drive genuine issues underground.

Grace and Firmness in Action

Once you've built this foundation of understanding and trust, there will still be times when gossip needs direct attention. When that happens, approaching it strategically rather than reactively works best. The goal isn't to humiliate or punish, but to redirect behavior and protect culture.

Stay calm and curious. Don't accuse; ask questions. "I've heard some concerns circulating. Can we talk about what's really happening?" This approach invites honesty rather than defensiveness.

Restoring What Gossip Has Broken

Even when following the patient, systematic approach recommended for new leaders, you may still inherit teams where gossip has already damaged relationships and eroded trust. People may have taken sides, reputations have been unfairly tarnished, or team members actively avoid each other. In these situations, prevention isn't enough—you need intentional restoration.

Acknowledge the damage without relitigating the past. "I know there have been some difficult dynamics on this team. We're not going to rehash every detail of what happened, but we are going to move forward differently." This validates people's experiences without getting trapped in he-said/she-said conversations.

Create opportunities for fresh starts. Sometimes this means restructuring how teams interact, changing meeting formats, or even shifting some responsibilities to give people space to rebuild trust gradually. The goal isn't to force instant friendship, but to create environments where professional respect can be reestablished.

Address lingering reputation damage directly. When someone's character or competence has been unfairly questioned through gossip, leaders may need to publicly clarify the record. "I want to be clear that the concerns raised about Sarah's project management have been thoroughly reviewed, and her work consistently meets our standards." This kind of clear communication helps restore credibility that whispers may have undermined.

Model vulnerability appropriately. Leaders who admit their own past mistakes with communication—without oversharing—give others permission to start fresh. "I haven't always handled conflict well in previous roles, but I'm committed to doing better here, and I hope we can all grow together."

Be patient with the process. Trust that took months or years to break won't be rebuilt in a few team meetings. Look for small signs of progress—people talking directly instead of through intermediaries, willingness to collaborate on projects, or simply showing up to meetings without visible tension. Celebrate these incremental victories without making a big production of them.

Remember that some relationships may never return to their original state, and that's okay. The goal is creating an environment where everyone can do their best work professionally, not forcing personal friendships that may no longer be possible.

Leading from Personal Experience

Leaders who have personally experienced the damage gossip can cause bring unique credibility to this challenge. Past pain becomes present wisdom when channeled appropriately.

Share stories strategically. Personal experience can help others understand why these issues matter, but avoid turning leadership platforms into therapy sessions. Focus on lessons learned rather than wounds endured.

Don't let negative experiences create oversuspicion. Each situation deserves fresh evaluation rather than assumptions based on past hurts. The goal is creating environments where everyone can thrive, not just protecting from further harm.

Building Something Better

The ultimate goal isn't just eliminating gossip—it's creating something better in its place. Healthy cultures are built on truth, respect, and shared accountability.

Focus on shared mission and meaningful goals. Teams that accomplish important work together have less energy for tearing each other down. Keep people focused on collective success rather than individual competition.

When someone makes a mistake, whether in gossip or any other area, focus on learning and growth rather than just correction. This creates safety for honesty and accountability.

Your Assignment as a Leader

Leadership isn't about perfection—it's about intention and consistency. It's about creating spaces where people can do their best work without fear, where conflicts get resolved through conversation rather than speculation, and where respect becomes a lived reality rather than just a poster on the wall.

Your commitment to building healthy environments may face resistance, but it's work worth doing. The environments you create today will shape the leaders of tomorrow. The peace you've found in the midst of chaos becomes the foundation for cultures where truth flourishes and gossip struggles to survive.

The internal transformation you've experienced—from someone controlled by others' opinions to someone anchored in unshakeable truth—now positions you to help others find that same security. Your leadership becomes a gift to those still learning to navigate difficult relationships and toxic dynamics.

"That person is like a tree planted by streams of water, which yields its fruit in season and whose leaf does not wither—whatever they do prospers" (Psalm 1:3).

The peace you've cultivated, the boundaries you've learned to create, and the confidence you've built in God's truth don't just protect you—they overflow into every environment you enter. Whether you're leading a team, raising a family, participating in community organizations, or simply living your daily life, the transformation you've experienced becomes a gift that strengthens others.

The journey from surviving gossip attacks to finding unshakeable internal peace positions you to live with a different kind of confidence—not the brittle confidence that depends on external validation, but the deep confidence that comes from knowing who you are and Whose you are, regardless of what others say or do.

In the next chapter, we'll explore how to walk in this unshakeable confidence, the kind that remains steady regardless of external circumstances and becomes a beacon of hope for everyone around you.

Chapter 10: Walking in Unshakeable Confidence

There comes a moment in your journey through and beyond gossip attacks when you realize something profound has shifted. You feel different—not just protected or healed, but actually confident in a way you've never experienced before. You know who you are and you're not afraid to be that person, regardless of who approves or disapproves.

This transformation reveals a truth many people discover after surviving character assassination: the confidence that emerges from tested character is unshakeable in ways that natural self-assurance never is. When you've maintained your integrity under pressure, spoken truth when it was costly, and discovered that God's love remains constant even when human approval disappears, you develop an inner strength that external circumstances can't touch.

This isn't the confidence that comes from achievements, compliments, or favorable circumstances. This is the confidence that comes from knowing who you are when everything else is stripped away—and discovering that person is worth defending.

"But he knows the way that I take; when he has tested me, I will come forth as gold" (Job 23:10).

Understanding True Confidence vs. External Validation

The confidence our culture promotes is often built on shifting foundations: how we look, what we accomplish, who approves of us, how we compare to others. This type of confidence feels good when things are going well, but it crumbles under pressure because it depends on factors outside our control.

Going through gossip attacks exposes the difference between confidence built on external validation and confidence built on internal truth. When the external support disappears—when people question your motives, criticize your character, or withdraw their approval—you discover whether your sense of worth was anchored in their opinions or in something deeper.

The confidence that survives these attacks isn't built on external validation—it's built on internal truth. It's knowing that your worth was established by God before you accomplished anything or failed at anything. It's understanding that your identity is secure regardless of human opinion.

This isn't flattery or positive thinking—it's theological truth about your identity that doesn't change based on circumstances.

The Foundation: Knowing Whose You Are

The most profound shift in confidence comes when you stop trying to earn your worth and start remembering it was already established. You were chosen before the foundation of the world (Ephesians 1:4), loved with an everlasting love (Jeremiah 31:3), and accepted in the Beloved (Ephesians 1:6). These truths don't fluctuate based on workplace politics, family dynamics, or social approval.

When you anchor your confidence in your identity as God's beloved child, criticism becomes information to evaluate rather than attacks on your worth. Success becomes gratitude for opportunities rather than proof of value. Setbacks become learning experiences rather than evidence of inadequacy.

This foundation changes everything. Instead of walking through life seeking validation, you walk through life offering it. Instead of defending your worth, you demonstrate it through how you treat others and respond to challenges.

Building Confidence Through Tested Character

Every challenge you've navigated with integrity has built your resilience muscle. You've already proven you can handle difficult situations and come out stronger. The experiences that felt overwhelming in the moment have become testimonies of your ability to overcome obstacles with God's help.

Your past struggles have given you:

- Wisdom that only comes through experience

- Compassion for others facing similar challenges

- Strength you didn't know you possessed

- Proof that you can maintain your character under pressure

Instead of viewing difficult experiences as evidence of your inadequacy, begin seeing them as testimonies of your resilience. Ask yourself: What did I learn? How did I grow? What strength did I discover? What character qualities were developed through this trial?

"Consider it pure joy, my brothers and sisters, whenever you face trials of many kinds, because you know that the testing of your faith produces perseverance. Let perseverance finish its work so that you may be mature and complete, not lacking anything" (James 1:2-4).

These aren't just survival stories—they're victory testimonies that demonstrate God's faithfulness and your own resilience when anchored in His truth.

Confidence in Your Voice and Authority

One of the most powerful shifts in confidence comes when you realize your voice carries authority—not because of your position or credentials, but because truth spoken with love has inherent power.

You no longer need to apologize for having opinions or hedge every suggestion with qualifiers. When you speak from experience and wisdom, you can offer ideas with confidence while remaining open to other perspectives.

When someone questions your character or spreads false narratives, you have both the right and responsibility to speak truth clearly and calmly. Your response comes from strength, not defensiveness:

"That's not accurate, and I'm comfortable with who I am."

"If there's something to discuss about my work or behavior, I'm happy to be part of that conversation."

"I'd rather focus on building people up than discussing those who aren't here."

You're not explaining yourself for approval, you're speaking truth because truth matters and your peace is worth protecting.

"Therefore, having this ministry by the mercy of God, we do not lose heart. But we have renounced disgraceful, underhanded ways. We refuse to practice cunning or to tamper with God's word, but by the open statement of the truth we would

commend ourselves to everyone's conscience in the sight of God" (2 Corinthians 4:1-2, ESV).

Daily Practices That Build Unshakeable Confidence

Anchor in Scripture: Start each day reminding yourself of God's truth about your identity. Read verses that reinforce your worth: Philippians 4:13 for capability, Isaiah 40:31 for renewed strength, Romans 8:37 for victory. This isn't just morning devotions—it's daily identity reinforcement.

Practice Gratitude: Focus on what's going right in your life rather than what's lacking or difficult. Gratitude shifts your perspective from scarcity to abundance, from victim mentality to victor mindset.

"Give thanks in all circumstances; for this is God's will for you in Christ Jesus" *(1 Thessalonians 5:18).*

Pray with Confidence: Talk to God like the friend He is. Some days it's "Thank you for this opportunity to grow," other days it's "Give me strength for this challenge." Prayer isn't begging—it's accessing the resources of heaven as God's beloved child.

Speak Truth to Yourself: When negative thoughts arise, immediately counter them with truth. "I can't do anything right" becomes "I'm learning and growing." "Nobody likes me" becomes "God loves me and has placed people in my life who appreciate me."

"Finally, brothers and sisters, whatever is true, whatever is noble, whatever is right, whatever is pure, whatever is lovely, whatever is admirable—if anything is excellent or praiseworthy—think about such things" (Philippians 4:8).

Building Your Support Network

Confidence grows in community with people who see your true value and call out your best self. Be intentional about surrounding yourself with voices that build rather than tear down.

Seek relationships with people who:

- Celebrate your growth and cheer your progress

- Speak truth with love when you need redirection

- Demonstrate what confident living looks like

- Share your values and faith foundation

Distance yourself from relationships that consistently drain your energy or undermine your confidence. This isn't about pride or avoiding accountability—it's about wisdom in choosing influences that help you become who God created you to be.

Living as the Victor You Already Are

The confidence you're seeking isn't something you need to find—it's something you need to recognize. It's been within you all along, placed there by the One who created you for greatness and redeemed you for His glory.

You are not someone who survived difficult circumstances—you are someone who conquered them through Christ's strength. You are not recovering from your past—you are stepping boldly into the future Jesus has prepared for you. You are not hoping to find confidence someday—you are choosing to walk in it today because of who you are in Him.

The experiences that tried to destroy your confidence have actually equipped you with:

- Unshakeable faith in God's faithfulness

- Proven resilience that comes from testing

- Wisdom that can help others navigate their challenges

- A testimony of victory that points others to hope

From Confidence to Influence

As you walk in this unshakeable confidence, you become a living testimony to what's possible when someone anchors their identity in God's truth rather than human opinion. People notice when you stop seeking approval and start offering authentic leadership. They're drawn to the peace and security you carry.

This confidence isn't about becoming proud or dismissive of others. It's about being so secure in your own identity that you can:

- Genuinely celebrate others' successes without comparison

- Offer help without hidden agendas or expectation of return

- Speak truth without needing to defend your right to have opinions

- Listen to criticism without being destroyed by it

- Extend grace to those who haven't extended it to you

The confidence you've built through testing becomes the foundation for the influence you'll have in building healthier communities, supporting others through their battles, and creating environments where truth and grace flourish together.

Walking Forward with Unshakeable Security

This confidence isn't a destination—it's a way of living. Each day brings new opportunities to choose God's truth over human opinion, to respond from strength rather than react from insecurity, and to let your security in Christ overflow into every relationship and situation you encounter.

The journey that began with surviving gossip attacks has transformed you into someone who can thrive regardless of external circumstances. You've learned that true confidence doesn't depend on perfect conditions or universal approval—it depends on knowing Whose you are and walking in that truth daily.

"Being confident of this, that he who began a good work in you will carry it on to completion until the day of Christ Jesus" (Philippians 1:6).

The transformation is complete: you've moved from someone whose confidence was shaken by others' opinions to someone whose confidence is rooted in unchanging truth. You've learned that real confidence doesn't come from having all the answers or never facing criticism, it comes from knowing who you are regardless of external circumstances.

This unshakeable confidence becomes the foundation for everything else in your life. When you know your worth isn't up for debate, you can engage authentically in relationships without hidden agendas. When you trust your own judgment, you can make decisions based on wisdom rather than fear. When you're secure in God's love, you can extend grace to others from a position of strength rather than neediness.

Your confidence becomes a gift not just to yourself, but to everyone whose life you touch. In a world full of insecurity and comparison, you offer something different: the peaceful strength that comes from being rooted and grounded in love that never fails.

This confidence will serve you well as we explore one of the most challenging yet liberating aspects of your healing journey: learning to forgive those who wounded you while protecting yourself from further harm, and discovering how forgiveness becomes one of your greatest acts of strength rather than weakness.

Chapter 11: Forgiveness as an Act of Strength

The phone call you never expected might come someday—an apology from someone who participated in spreading gossip about you. Or perhaps it never will. Either way, you'll discover one of life's most powerful truths: forgiveness is never about the person who hurt you. It's about refusing to let their actions control your peace.

Many people who have survived character assassination find themselves preparing speeches for hypothetical confrontations, imagining what they'd say if given the chance to explain how much damage was caused. But when the moment for grace actually arrives, something unexpected often happens—you find yourself responding with compassion you didn't know you possessed, not because they deserve it, but because you need to be free.

This transformation doesn't happen overnight. Forgiveness isn't a single decision you make and move on from—it's a process that transforms you from the inside out, teaching you that forgiveness is never weakness. It's one of the strongest choices you can make.

Understanding What Forgiveness Really Is

Years ago, I experienced something that changed my understanding of forgiveness forever. In a moment when I was deeply hurt by someone's betrayal, something unexpected happened—a profound sense of peace came over me, so undeniable that I couldn't ignore it. It wasn't something I worked up or talked myself into. It was forgiveness, pure and simple, flowing through me like a gift I hadn't asked for but desperately needed.

In that moment, I realized forgiveness wasn't just something I could choose to do—it was something God was offering to do through me. The peace that accompanied it was unlike anything I'd experienced. It wasn't the absence of hurt; it was the presence of something greater than the hurt. The burden that had been weighing so heavily on me was lifted completely.

"Be kind and compassionate to one another, forgiving each other, just as in Christ God forgave you" (Ephesians 4:32). "Bear with each other and forgive one another if any of you has a grievance against someone. Forgive as the Lord forgave you" (Colossians 3:13).

Forgiveness is:

- A choice to release resentment for your own freedom

- Deciding their actions will no longer control your emotions

- Protecting your heart from ongoing bitterness

- Trusting God to handle justice while you focus on healing

- Recognizing it as a gift from God that you give yourself

Forgiveness is not:

- Saying what they did was acceptable

- Forgetting what happened or pretending it didn't hurt

- Automatically rebuilding the relationship to previous levels of intimacy

- Putting yourself back in harmful situations

- Requiring their apology or acknowledgment

As Matthew 6:14-15 reminds us, choosing to forgive others opens us to receiving forgiveness from God. You can forgive someone completely while still maintaining healthy boundaries. Forgiveness and wisdom often go hand in hand.

The Biblical Foundation: How God's Forgiveness Empowers Ours

Understanding how to forgive others begins with understanding how God forgives us. His forgiveness isn't based on our performance, our apologies, or our promises to do better. It's based on His character and His love, demonstrated through Christ's sacrifice on the cross.

"But God demonstrates his own love for us in this: While we were still sinners, Christ died for us" (Romans 5:8).

When we grasp the magnitude of God's forgiveness toward us—complete, unconditional, and costly—it changes our perspective on forgiving others. We don't forgive because people deserve it or because they've earned it. We forgive because we've been forgiven, and that forgiveness flows through us to others.

This doesn't make forgiveness easy, but it makes it possible. When you feel like you can't forgive someone, remember that you're not being asked to manufacture forgiveness from your own strength. You're being invited to let God's forgiveness flow through you.

"And when you stand praying, if you hold anything against anyone, forgive them, so that your Father in heaven may forgive you your sins" (Mark 11:25).

The Cost of Unforgiveness

Before exploring how to forgive, it's important to understand what unforgiveness costs you. Holding onto bitterness and resentment doesn't punish the person who hurt you—it punishes you.

Spiritually, unforgiveness creates a barrier between you and God. It's difficult to receive grace when you're unwilling to extend it. Your prayers feel hollow, worship feels forced, and peace remains elusive.

Emotionally, carrying resentment is like carrying a heavy backpack filled with rocks. It weighs you down, makes every step harder, and leaves you exhausted. You may find yourself replaying conversations, planning confrontations, or feeling angry at unexpected moments.

Physically, research has shown that harboring grudges can contribute to stress, high blood pressure, weakened immune systems, and sleep problems. Your body pays the price for your emotional burden.

Relationally, unforgiveness often spills over into other relationships. You may find yourself suspicious, defensive, or unable to trust. The hurt from one person begins affecting your ability to connect with everyone else.

"In your anger do not sin: Do not let the sun go down while you are still angry, and do not give the devil a foothold" (Ephesians 4:26-27).

The cost of unforgiveness is too high to pay. It gives the people who hurt you continued power over your peace, your relationships, and your spiritual health.

The Process: From Decision to Freedom

Forgiveness is both a decision and a process. You can choose to begin forgiving even when your emotions aren't ready, and work through the feelings over time.

Step 1: Acknowledge the Reality

Don't minimize what happened or rush to "get over it." Honest acknowledgment of the hurt is necessary before healing can begin. You can't forgive what you won't face honestly. Write down specifically what happened and how it affected you—your reputation, your relationships, your confidence, your peace.

Step 2: Make the Decision

Forgiveness begins with a choice, not a feeling. You may not feel ready emotionally, but you can decide: "I choose to begin the process of forgiving [specific person], even though I'm still hurt by what they did." This isn't about feeling differently immediately—it's about choosing a direction.

Step 3: Surrender Through Prayer

Bring the situation to God in prayer. Ask for His help in releasing the resentment and finding peace. Sometimes we need divine strength to do what feels impossible in our own power.

"Cast all your anxiety on him because he cares for you" (1 Peter 5:7).

A prayer might be: "God, I can't do this on my own. Help me release this anger and see this person through Your eyes. Give me the strength to forgive as You have forgiven me."

Step 4: Release Through Declaration

Speak your forgiveness out loud, even if they can't hear you. Say: "I forgive [specific name] for [specific actions]. I release them from the debt they owe me. I choose my freedom over holding onto this resentment."

This declaration isn't about them—it's about you choosing freedom. You're not saying their actions were acceptable; you're saying those actions will no longer control your peace.

Step 5: Redirect Your Energy

Take all the mental and emotional energy you've been spending on resentment and channel it toward your purpose, growth, and the people who deserve your focus. This is where forgiveness becomes practical—choosing to invest in life-giving activities rather than life-draining bitterness.

When There's No Apology

Many people struggle with forgiving when the person who hurt them shows no remorse, offers no apology, and may even continue their harmful behavior. The absence of acknowledgment can make forgiveness feel impossible or even wrong.

But forgiveness doesn't require the other person's participation. Jesus demonstrated this on the cross when He said, "Father, forgive them, for they do not know what they are doing" (Luke 23:34). He didn't wait for apologies or changed behavior—He forgave while they were still in the act of crucifying Him.

When there's no apology:

- Remember that forgiveness is for your freedom, not their benefit

- Accept that they may never acknowledge the harm they caused

- Focus on releasing your resentment rather than changing their heart

- Trust God to deal with their conscience and consequences

- Protect yourself through boundaries while still choosing forgiveness

"If it is possible, as far as it depends on you, live at peace with everyone" (Romans 12:18).

Notice the phrase "as far as it depends on you." You can only control your part of the equation. Choose peace and forgiveness regardless of their response.

The Challenge of Forgiving Yourself

Often the hardest person to forgive is yourself. When you've been through gossip attacks, you may replay the situation endlessly, wondering if you could have handled things differently, said something better, or prevented the whole situation.

Self-condemnation sounds like:

- "If I had just kept my mouth shut..."
- "I should have seen this coming"
- "Maybe if I had been more careful..."
- "I brought this on myself"

This internal criticism can be more damaging than the original attack. You become your own harshest critic, holding yourself to standards of perfection you'd never expect from others.

Self-forgiveness involves:

- Acknowledging your mistakes without excusing them
- Learning from what happened without being crushed by it
- Accepting that you did the best you could with what you knew at the time
- Choosing growth over guilt
- Remembering that God's mercy covers your failures through Christ

If Jesus already paid the price for your mistakes, making Him pay twice by refusing to accept His forgiveness is actually prideful, not humble. Extend the same grace to yourself that you're willing to give others.

Protecting Your Peace Through Boundaries

Forgiving someone doesn't mean removing all boundaries. In fact, healthy boundaries often become more important after forgiveness, not less. You can forgive your difficult family member while limiting how much access they have to your emotional space.

Boundaries after forgiveness might include:

- Limiting contact or communication

- Refusing to engage in certain conversations

- Protecting your energy by stepping away when necessary

- Being kind but not vulnerable

- Maintaining emotional distance while showing basic respect

When people question your boundaries after forgiveness, you can respond: "Forgiveness doesn't mean returning to unhealthy patterns. I can forgive someone and still protect my peace."

Remember: boundaries aren't walls built from bitterness—they're gates you control from a place of wisdom and self-respect.

When Forgiveness Feels Impossible

Some situations feel too painful, too fresh, or too ongoing to forgive. When you're dealing with repeated harm or public humiliation, forgiveness can seem like an impossible demand.

In these situations, forgiveness becomes a daily choice rather than a one-time decision. Some days you'll feel forgiving, other days you'll have to choose forgiveness despite your feelings. This is where the decision part of forgiveness becomes crucial—you're not waiting to feel ready, you're choosing freedom regardless of your emotions.

When forgiveness feels impossible:

- Start with a willingness to be willing: "God, I don't want to forgive them, but I want to want to"

- Pray for small steps: "Help me release just a little of this resentment today"

- Focus on your freedom rather than their behavior

- Remember that forgiveness is a process, not perfection

- Seek support from trusted friends, counselors, or spiritual mentors

Daily forgiveness prayers might sound like: "God, I don't feel forgiving today, but I choose to release [name] again. Help me see them the way You see them. Heal my heart and protect my peace."

"If your brother or sister sins against you, rebuke them; and if they repent, forgive them. Even if they sin against you seven times in a day and seven times come back to you saying 'I repent,' you must forgive them" (Luke 17:3-4).

The Freedom That Follows

The peace that comes from genuine forgiveness is unlike any other freedom you'll experience. It's like setting down a heavy weight you didn't realize you were still carrying. When you're no longer carrying the burden of resentment, you discover energy you'd forgotten you had.

Forgiveness creates space for:

- The life you're meant to live

- Energy for your purpose, relationships, and dreams

- Love without fear of being hurt again

- Trust balanced with wisdom

- Engagement from strength rather than fear

- Focus on your future instead of being trapped by your past

- Confidence that you can handle whatever comes your way

This freedom allows you to walk into new relationships and opportunities without the baggage of past hurts coloring every interaction. You become someone who can love openly while staying wise, trust appropriately while maintaining boundaries, and engage authentically without hidden agendas.

The Ripple Effect of Grace

When you choose forgiveness, you often inspire others to do the same. Your choice to respond with grace instead of bitterness becomes a powerful testimony to the transformative power of God's love working through human weakness.

People notice when you stop being defensive, when you treat difficult people with consistent kindness, and when you handle conflict with grace. Your forgiveness doesn't just free you, it creates space for others to experience grace and find their own freedom from bitterness.

Your choice to forgive becomes:

- A testimony to the power of grace

- An invitation for others to find freedom from resentment

- A demonstration that healing is possible

- A model of strength rather than weakness

- A reflection of God's character in human form

Moving Forward in Freedom

The confident, purposeful life you're building has no room for the weight of unforgiveness. Release it, and step into the freedom that's waiting for you. Remember that forgiveness is ultimately about your relationship with God and your own spiritual health, not about the person who hurt you.

As you walk in this freedom, you become living proof that it's possible to be wounded but not broken, hurt but not hardened, damaged but not destroyed. Your ability to forgive becomes one of your greatest testimonies to God's grace and one of your most powerful tools for building healthy relationships going forward.

"Get rid of all bitterness, rage and anger, brawling and slander, along with every form of malice. Be kind and compassionate to one another, forgiving each other, just as in Christ God forgave you" (Ephesians 4:31-32).

The journey from victim to victor includes this crucial stop at forgiveness—not as a destination, but as a doorway to the fullness of life God has planned for you. When you walk through that doorway, you carry with you the wisdom you've gained, the strength you've built, and the grace you've experienced.

Forgiveness transforms you from someone controlled by past hurts into someone empowered by present choices. This transformation becomes the foundation for everything that follows—deeper relationships, greater influence, unshakeable peace, and the kind of life that reflects God's redemptive power in every area.

With forgiveness as your final act of strength in this healing journey, you're now ready to step boldly into your future, carrying forward all you've learned and become. The path ahead is no longer defined by what was done to you, but by who you've chosen to become through it all.

Chapter 12: Moving Forward

After walking through the process of healing and forgiveness, you reach a crossroads that will define the rest of your story. You can stay where you are, comfortable in your recovery but still defined by what happened to you. Or you can step forward into something new—a life that honors what you've learned without being limited by what you've endured.

This crossroads is sacred ground. It's where victimhood transforms into victory, where survival becomes thriving, and where your painful past becomes the foundation for a purposeful future.

Moving forward doesn't mean forgetting the past or pretending the wounds never existed. It means choosing to build your future on the foundation of who you've become through the healing process rather than who you were when the attacks began.

"Forget the former things; do not dwell on the past. See, I am doing a new thing! Now it springs up; do you not perceive it? I am making a way in the wilderness and streams in the wasteland" (Isaiah 43:18-19).

The Choice Before You

Standing at this crossroads, you face a fundamental choice about your identity going forward. Will you be someone who survived gossip attacks, or will you be someone whose character was refined through trials? Will you live defensively, constantly protecting against future hurt, or will you live purposefully, using your strength to build something beautiful?

The difference isn't semantic—it's transformational. One identity keeps you tethered to the past; the other launches you into the future God has prepared for you.

You now possess wisdom that only comes through testing, compassion that only develops through suffering, strength that only emerges through pressure, and discernment that only sharpens through experience. These aren't consolation prizes for what you've endured—they're the very qualities that position you to impact others' lives in ways you never could have before.

"And we know that in all things God works for the good of those who love him, who have been called according to his purpose" (Romans 8:28).

Your trials weren't pointless suffering. They were preparation for influence you couldn't have had any other way.

Anchoring Your Peace Intentionally

True peace doesn't come from managing your circumstances or controlling your environment. It comes from Jesus.

This isn't the temporary peace that comes from having everything go your way. It's the deep, unshakeable peace that remains steady even when external circumstances are chaotic. It's the peace that allows you to sleep soundly even when storms rage around you because you know whose you are, regardless of what others are saying.

Daily peace protection requires:

Morning anchoring - Begin each day connecting with God before engaging with the world's demands. Let His truth about your identity be the first voice you hear, not the chaos of news, social media, or yesterday's worries.

Thought evaluation - When anxiety or old patterns try to resurface, immediately bring them to the One who can calm every storm. The battle for inner peace is often won or lost in your thought life.

Evening release - End each day by releasing any tension or negativity you've absorbed. Forgive again if needed. Express gratitude for God's faithfulness. Rest in His promises rather than tomorrow's uncertainties.

Peace isn't something that just appears and stays forever, it requires intentional cultivation and protection. But you now have the tools and experience to guard what matters most.

Evaluating What Deserves Your Energy

One of the most valuable skills developed through surviving gossip attacks is learning to evaluate what truly deserves your emotional investment. Not every conversation, conflict, or crisis requires your full engagement.

Before reacting to situations or investing deeply in relationships, run them through an internal filter:

- Does this support my peace or disrupt it?

- Will engaging in this help me grow or drain me further?

- Are the people involved showing patterns of respect or patterns of manipulation?

- Does this align with my values and goals, or is it just familiar drama?

- Am I responding from wisdom or reacting from old wounds?

This evaluation isn't about becoming cold or distant. It's about becoming wise with your emotional resources. Your energy is finite and valuable—it should be invested in people and pursuits that honor your growth and contribute to your purpose.

"Above all else, guard your heart, for everything you do flows from it" (Proverbs 4:23).

You've learned that caring about people doesn't mean carrying their problems, and loving someone doesn't require absorbing their emotional chaos.

Living From Your Values, Not Your Wounds

When you're in survival mode, most choices are reactions—protecting yourself from further harm, avoiding situations that trigger painful memories, or responding defensively to perceived threats. But as you heal and grow stronger, you can begin making proactive choices based on who you want to become rather than what you want to avoid.

Values-based living means:

Choosing integrity over image - Prioritizing who you really are over how others perceive you

Pursuing authenticity over approval - Being genuine even when it would be easier to wear a mask

Valuing depth over breadth - Building fewer but more meaningful relationships rather than seeking universal acceptance

Following purpose over safety - Taking appropriate risks to fulfill your calling rather than playing it safe

Practicing courage over comfort - Doing what's right even when it's difficult

The shift from wound-driven to value-driven living is profound. Instead of asking "How can I avoid getting hurt again?" you start asking "What would courage and integrity look like here?" Instead of "What will they think?" you ask "What does God think?" Instead of "How can I stay safe?" you ask "How can I serve faithfully?"

"Trust in the Lord with all your heart and lean not on your own understanding; in all your ways submit to him, and he will make your paths straight" (Proverbs 3:5-6).

Creating Environments That Reflect Your Growth

As you move forward, you naturally begin creating and seeking environments that reflect the health you've developed internally. This might mean changes in your social circles, workplace dynamics, church involvement, or family interactions.

You become less tolerant of toxic communication patterns—not in a harsh or judgmental way, but with a quiet confidence that refuses to participate. When conversations turn to gossip, you redirect or remove yourself. When people try to pull you into drama, you maintain boundaries. When environments consistently undermine your peace, you limit your exposure or find alternatives.

This transformation looks like:

In relationships - Focusing on building connections with people who share your values and demonstrate character, while maintaining appropriate boundaries with those who don't

In work - Pursuing excellence while refusing to participate in office politics or toxic communication patterns

In family - Staying connected to people you enjoy while setting gentle boundaries with difficult relatives

In community - Contributing positively while declining involvement in negativity or gossip

You're not trying to manage everyone's emotions anymore. You stay connected to people who add life to your relationships and create healthy distance from those who consistently drain your energy.

"Do not be yoked together with unbelievers. For what do righteousness and wickedness have in common? Or what fellowship can light have with darkness?" (2 Corinthians 6:14).

This doesn't mean isolation from anyone who isn't perfect, it means wisdom about the level of intimacy and influence you allow from different people in your life.

Facing Common Fears About Moving Forward

"What if I get hurt again?" You probably will face difficulties again—that's part of life. But you now know you can survive and even thrive through challenges. You have tools, wisdom, and most importantly, a relationship with God that sustains you through any storm.

"What if people don't accept the 'new me'?" Some people won't. They were comfortable with the old version of you that was easier to control or manipulate. Your growth threatens their dysfunction. This is information about them, not about you. The right people will celebrate your transformation.

"What if I make mistakes or fall back into old patterns?" You will make mistakes—that's how humans learn and grow. The difference now is that mistakes don't define you or derail you. You have the skills to recognize when you're slipping, correct course, and continue moving forward.

"What if my purpose isn't as significant as I hope?" God doesn't call you to change the entire world—He calls you to faithfully steward the gifts, relationships, and opportunities He places in front of you. Your "small" influence may impact generations in ways you never see.

"For I know the plans I have for you," declares the Lord, "plans to prosper you and not to harm you, to give you hope and a future" (Jeremiah 29:11).

Discovering Purpose Beyond the Pain

Your trials have developed character, wisdom, and compassion that can serve others, but your identity and calling extend far beyond what you've suffered. The ultimate goal of moving forward isn't just recovery, it's discovering and living the purpose that exists beyond your painful experiences.

Your transformed life might include:

Leadership opportunities - Using the skills you developed navigating toxic environments to create healthier cultures

Mentoring relationships - Guiding others through challenges you've already conquered

Creative expression - Rediscovering parts of yourself that got buried under survival mode

Ministry calling - Serving God and others from the overflow of His grace in your life

Career advancement - Pursuing opportunities with confidence rooted in proven resilience

Deeper relationships - Building connections based on mutual respect and shared values

But you also rediscover parts of yourself that existed before the attacks—dreams, gifts, interests, and callings that got buried under the weight of survival. As you heal, these begin to resurface, and you realize your life has purposes that have nothing to do with what you've overcome.

Building a Legacy of Grace

Your transformation creates ripple effects that extend far beyond your own healing. The way you've chosen to respond to injustice, extend forgiveness, and maintain integrity under pressure becomes a testimony that influences everyone who observes your journey.

Your legacy might include:

Breaking generational cycles - Modeling healthy conflict resolution for your children and family

Creating cultural change - Influencing workplace, church, or community environments toward greater health

Mentoring transformation - Helping others navigate their own healing journeys

Demonstrating grace - Showing that it's possible to be wounded without becoming bitter

Living with purpose - Inspiring others to pursue their callings despite past pain

The environments you create, the relationships you build, and the example you set become gifts to future generations who will benefit from the health you've chosen to cultivate.

"A good person leaves an inheritance for their children's children" (Proverbs *13:22*).

This inheritance isn't just financial—it's the spiritual and emotional health that gets passed down through families and communities.

Embracing Your Future With Unshakeable Confidence

Moving forward ultimately means embracing an uncertain future with confidence—not confidence in your ability to control outcomes, but confidence in God's goodness and in your own capacity to handle whatever comes.

You've already survived what felt like the worst-case scenario. You've been misunderstood, attacked, isolated, and wounded, and you're still standing. This doesn't make you immune to future pain, but it does prove your resilience and God's faithfulness.

The confidence you carry now is different from any confidence you had before the trials began. It's tested confidence, proven through fire. It's not based on avoiding difficulty but on knowing you can walk through difficulty with grace.

This confidence allows you to:

Take appropriate risks - In relationships, career, ministry, and creative endeavors

Love without fear - Knowing you can survive disappointment if it comes

Lead with authenticity - No longer needing to pretend or perform for acceptance

Speak truth boldly - Confident that your worth isn't determined by others' responses

Pursue your calling - Regardless of who understands or approves

Your Next Steps Forward

Immediate actions you can take:

1. **Write your vision** - Document what you want your transformed life to look like in relationships, career, service, and personal growth

2. **Identify your values** - List the principles that will guide your decisions going forward

3. **Assess your environments** - Evaluate which relationships and situations support your growth versus those that hinder it

4. **Set new goals** - Based on your gifts and calling, not just healing from past wounds

5. **Find your community** - Connect with people who share your values and can support your continued growth

6. **Begin serving** - Use your experience to help others, even in small ways

7. **Keep growing** - Continue learning, developing your gifts, and deepening your relationship with God

Writing Your New Chapter

The chapter of your life that was dominated by others' opinions and attacks is closing. The new chapter beginning is one you write from a place of security, wisdom, and unshakeable confidence in whose you are.

You move forward not as someone running from a painful past, but as someone walking confidently toward a future full of purpose and growth. The people who couldn't see your value don't get to determine your destiny. The voices that tried to tear you down don't get to write your story's conclusion.

You are not the same person who was first attacked by gossip and lies. You are refined by trials but not defined by them, strengthened by struggle but not stuck in it. You have been transformed from victim to victor, from survivor to thriver, from wounded to whole.

The future stretching out before you is not limited by your past but empowered by your growth. God has plans for you that are good, plans that give you hope and a future that exceeds what you could have imagined when you were in the midst of the storm.

Your story of transformation now becomes a beacon of hope for others who are still in their storms, still believing the lies, still wondering if healing is possible. You are living proof that it is—not just possible, but promised to all who trust in Him.

Step boldly into that future. The best chapters of your story are still being written, and the Author of your life never wastes a single page of pain in service of the masterpiece He's creating in and through you.

Conclusion

As we reach the end of this journey together, I want you to understand something profound: you are not the same person who started reading this book. The very act of engaging with these concepts, wrestling with these truths, and choosing to seek healing rather than remain trapped in victimhood has changed you.

You may not feel completely transformed yet—healing is a process, not an event—but the seeds of change have been planted. The knowledge you've gained cannot be unlearned. The tools you've discovered cannot be taken away. The truth you've encountered about your worth and identity will continue to grow stronger, even when circumstances try to convince you otherwise.

The Choice That Changes Everything

Throughout this book, we've returned again and again to one central question: Whose voice do you follow? This isn't just about surviving gossip attacks, it's the daily choice that determines whether you live in freedom or bondage, peace or anxiety, purpose or reactivity.

Every morning you wake up, you're presented with competing voices vying for your attention and allegiance. The voice of gossip still whispers lies about your worth, trying to convince you that others' opinions define your value. The voice of fear still warns of worst-case scenarios, encouraging you to live defensively rather than purposefully. The voice of past wounds still tries to make decisions for you, keeping you trapped in old patterns.

But now you know there's another voice—clearer, truer, and more reliable than all the others. It's the voice of the One who knew you before you were born, who chose you before the foundation of the world, who loves you with an everlasting love that cannot be diminished by human opinion or circumstance.

"My sheep listen to my voice; I know them, and they follow me. I give them eternal life, and they shall never perish; no one will snatch them out of my hand" (John 10:27-28).

What You've Learned

Through this journey, you've learned that gossip is far more destructive than casual chatter—it systematically dismantles trust, community, and individual wellbeing. Understanding its various disguises helps you recognize and refuse participation in communication patterns that harm rather than heal.

You've learned to respond to attacks with wisdom rather than reactivity, understanding that immediate defense often backfires and that strategic patience coupled with consistent character is more powerful than desperate self-justification.

You've built spiritual resilience by understanding that some battles require more than human solutions. The armor of God isn't just metaphorical—it's practical equipment for surviving attacks on your reputation, relationships, and sense of reality.

You've created boundaries that protect without isolating, understanding the difference between healthy self-protection and bitter withdrawal from all relationships.

You've discovered that peace doesn't depend on perfect circumstances but on connecting with the source of peace Himself. True peace remains steady even when external chaos continues.

You've worked through the difficult process of forgiveness and healing, learning that releasing others from your judgment frees you to live fully in your purpose rather than remaining trapped in their story.

"And the peace of God, which transcends all understanding, will guard your hearts and your minds in Christ Jesus" (Philippians 4:7).

The Ripple Effect of Your Healing

Your healing doesn't just affect you—it impacts everyone within your sphere of influence. The transformation that has taken place in your life creates healthier environments wherever you go. Your newfound peace during difficult interactions teaches others that it's possible to navigate conflict with grace. Your wisdom in handling challenges shows people around you how to maintain integrity under pressure.

The children in your life are watching how you navigate difficulty. They're learning from your example whether conflicts can be resolved with integrity or whether survival requires compromising your character. Your healing teaches them that it's possible to be wounded without becoming bitter, to be attacked without becoming defensive, to be misunderstood without losing your sense of self.

Your story becomes a source of hope for others walking similar paths. Your journey proves that healing and healthy relationships are possible. Your example shows that you can maintain your values while loving difficult people.

"Let your light shine before others, that they may see your good deeds and glorify your Father in heaven" (Matthew 5:16).

The Ongoing Journey

This book's end doesn't mark the completion of your healing—it marks your graduation to a new level of living. You now have tools that will serve you for the rest of your life, but like any tools, they require ongoing use and refinement.

There will be times when old wounds try to reopen, when new conflicts arise, or when you face different types of challenges that test what you've learned. This doesn't mean you've failed or that your healing isn't real. It means you're human, and the growth process continues throughout life.

You may find yourself helping others through similar struggles, using your hard-won wisdom to guide them toward healing. But remember the boundaries you've learned—you can support without rescuing, encourage without becoming enmeshed, and share your story without reliving your trauma.

"Brothers and sisters, if someone is caught in a sin, you who live by the Spirit should restore that person gently. But watch yourselves, or you also may be tempted" (Galatians 6:1).

Living Your New Chapter

As you close this book and step into whatever comes next, remember that you're not returning to your old life with better coping mechanisms. You're entering a new chapter with a transformed understanding of who you are and whose you are.

This new chapter isn't guaranteed to be free from conflict or challenge, but it will be marked by your ability to face whatever comes with grace, wisdom, and unshakeable confidence in God's goodness and sovereignty over your life.

You'll make decisions based on your values rather than your fears. You'll build relationships based on mutual respect and shared values rather than desperate need for approval. You'll pursue purposes that align with your gifts and God's calling rather than settling for whatever feels safe.

"Therefore, if anyone is in Christ, the new creation has come: The old has gone, the new is here!" (2 Corinthians 5:17).

Your Assignment Going Forward

Your story of surviving gossip and character assassination has prepared you for assignments you cannot yet see. The character you've developed through the refining fire will serve purposes beyond what you can currently imagine. The wisdom you've gained will benefit people whose names you don't yet know.

You are called to:

Walk in your identity - Live as someone defined by God's truth rather than human opinion

Create healthy environments - Use your influence to build cultures where gossip struggles to survive and authentic relationships can flourish

Speak truth in love - Address conflicts with grace while maintaining your integrity

Trust God with your reputation - Focus on stewarding your character while leaving your public image in His hands

Guide others to freedom - Share your wisdom with those still trapped in cycles of toxic communication

"For we are God's handiwork, created in Christ Jesus to do good works, which God prepared in advance for us to do" (Ephesians 2:10).

Final Words

You are not a victim of your circumstances—you are a victor through Christ who strengthens you. You are not defined by what others have said about you—you are defined by what God says about you. You are not limited by what you've overcome—you are empowered by who you've become through overcoming it.

The voice you choose to follow will continue to shape every aspect of your life. Choose wisely. Choose consistently. Choose the voice of truth, love, and eternal purpose.

Your best chapters are still being written. Your greatest contributions are still ahead of you. Your deepest joy and strongest impact await in the life that emerges on the other side of this refining process.

Go forward in peace. Walk confidently in your calling. Live fully in the freedom that comes from knowing whose you are.

The journey continues, but now you walk it with wisdom, strength, and unshakeable hope in the One whose voice matters most.

"Now to him who is able to do immeasurably more than all we ask or imagine, according to his power that is at work within us, to him be glory in the church and in Christ Jesus throughout all generations, for ever and ever! Amen" (Ephesians 3:20-21).

Self-Reflection Questions

Understanding Your Experience

1. Looking back at your experience with gossip or toxic communication, what warning signs did you miss or dismiss? What would you recognize more quickly now?

2. Which of the gossip "masks" have you encountered most frequently? How might recognizing these patterns change your responses going forward?

3. What voices have had the most influence over your sense of worth and identity? How do these compare to what God says about you?

Assessing Your Response Patterns

4. When faced with conflict or criticism, do you tend to react defensively, withdraw completely, or respond strategically? What drives these patterns?

5. Which piece of spiritual armor do you most need to "put on" daily? Why?

6. How do you currently handle information about others? Are there areas where you need to establish better boundaries around gossip?

Evaluating Your Relationships and Environment

7. Using the three-circle relationship model, who belongs in each circle of your life right now? Are there any adjustments you need to make?

8. What environments or relationships consistently drain your peace versus those that restore it? What changes might honor your healing?

9. If you're in a leadership position, what specific steps could you take to create a more gossip-resistant culture?

Exploring Forgiveness and Healing

10. Is there someone you need to forgive? What's holding you back, and what would freedom look like?

11. What lies about yourself have you believed as a result of others' words or actions? How can you replace these with God's truth?

12. How has your experience with gossip or betrayal changed your capacity for empathy toward others facing similar struggles?

Moving Forward with Purpose

13. What strengths, wisdom, or character qualities have you developed through your difficult experiences? How might God want to use these?

14. What dreams, gifts, or purposes existed before your painful experience that you might be ready to rediscover?

15. How would your life look different if you consistently chose to follow God's voice over human opinion? What specific changes would you make?

Daily Practice and Growth

16. What daily practices help you maintain spiritual and emotional health? Are there new habits you'd like to establish?

17. When you imagine yourself five years from now, walking in complete freedom from others' opinions, what do you see? What steps can you take toward that vision?

18. How can you use your story to help others without sacrificing your own wellbeing?

Final Reflection

19. Complete this statement: "The most important thing I've learned about whose voice to follow is..."

20. What is one specific action you will take this week to apply what you've learned from this book?

Scripture for Meditation and Memorization

Identity and Worth

- Psalm 139:14 - "I praise you because I am fearfully and wonderfully made; your works are wonderful, I know that full well."

- Ephesians 1:4 - "For he chose us in him before the creation of the world to be holy and blameless in his sight."

- 1 John 3:1 - "See what great love the Father has lavished on us, that we should be called children of God! And that is what we are!"

- Jeremiah 29:11 - "For I know the plans I have for you,' declares the Lord, 'plans to prosper you and not to harm you, to give you hope and a future.'"

Peace and Protection

- John 14:27 - "Peace I leave with you; my peace I give you. I do not give to you as the world gives. Do not let your hearts be troubled and do not be afraid."

- Psalm 46:10 - "Be still, and know that I am God; I will be exalted among the nations, I will be exalted in the earth."

- Isaiah 54:17 - "No weapon forged against you will prevail, and you will refute every tongue that accuses you. This is the heritage of the servants of the Lord, and this is their vindication from me,' declares the Lord."

- Psalm 31:19-20 - "How abundant are the good things that you have stored up for those who fear you... In the shelter of your presence you hide them from all human intrigues; in your dwelling you keep them safe from accusing tongues."

Strength and Confidence

- Philippians 4:13 - "I can do all this through him who gives me strength."

- Isaiah 40:31 - "But those who hope in the Lord will renew their strength. They will soar on wings like eagles; they will run and not grow weary, they will walk and not be faint."

- Romans 8:37 - "No, in all these things we are more than conquerors through him who loved us."

- 2 Timothy 1:7 - "For the Spirit God gave us does not make us timid, but gives us power, love and self-discipline."

Wisdom and Discernment

- Proverbs 3:5-6 - "Trust in the Lord with all your heart and lean not on your own understanding; in all your ways submit to him, and he will make your paths straight."

- James 1:5 - "If any of you lacks wisdom, you should ask God, who gives generously to all without finding fault, and it will be given to you."

- Proverbs 27:17 - "As iron sharpens iron, so one person sharpens another."

Forgiveness and Healing

- Matthew 6:14-15 - "For if you forgive other people when they sin against you, your heavenly Father will also forgive you. But if you do not forgive others their sins, your Father will not forgive your sins."

- Ephesians 4:32 - "Be kind and compassionate to one another, forgiving each other, just as in Christ God forgave you."

- Isaiah 61:3 - "...to bestow on them a crown of beauty instead of ashes, the oil of joy instead of mourning, and a garment of praise instead of a spirit of despair."

God's Justice and Vindication

- Romans 12:19 - "Do not take revenge, my dear friends, but leave room for God's wrath, for it is written: 'It is mine to avenge; I will repay,' says the Lord."

- Psalm 37:6 - "He will make your righteous reward shine like the dawn, your vindication like the noonday sun."

- Proverbs 26:20 - "Without wood a fire goes out; without a gossip a quarrel dies down."

Communication and Relationships

- Ephesians 4:29 - "Do not let any unwholesome talk come out of your mouths, but only what is helpful for building others up according to their needs, that it may benefit those who listen."

- Matthew 18:15 - "If your brother or sister sins, go and point out their fault, just between the two of you. If they listen to you, you have won them over."

- Romans 12:18 - "If it is possible, as far as it depends on you, live at peace with everyone."

Scripture References

Old Testament

Deuteronomy

- 19:15 - "A matter must be established by the testimony of two or three witnesses"

- 31:6 - "Be strong and courageous. Do not be afraid or terrified because of them, for the Lord your God goes with you; he will never leave you nor forsake you"

Joshua

- 1:9 - "Be strong and courageous. Do not be afraid; do not be discouraged, for the Lord your God will be with you wherever you go"

1 Kings

- 19:4-8 - Elijah under the broom tree receiving God's care and gentle whisper

Job

- 23:10 - "But he knows the way that I take; when he has tested me, I will come forth as gold"

Psalms

- 1:3 - "That person is like a tree planted by streams of water, which yields its fruit in season and whose leaf does not wither—whatever they do prospers"

- 31:13 - "For I hear many whispering, 'Terror on every side!' as they scheme together against me, as they plot to take my life"

- 31:19-20 - "How abundant are the good things that you have stored up for those who fear you... In the shelter of your presence you hide them from all human intrigues; in your dwelling you keep them safe from accusing tongues"

- 34:18 - "The Lord is close to the brokenhearted and saves those who are crushed in spirit"

- 46:10 - "Be still, and know that I am God"

- 64:3 - "They sharpen their tongues like swords and aim cruel words like deadly arrows"

- 91:4 - "He will cover you with his feathers, and under his wings you will find refuge; his faithfulness will be your shield and rampart"

- 139:14 - "I praise you because I am fearfully and wonderfully made; your works are wonderful, I know that full well"

Proverbs

- 4:23 - "Above all else, guard your heart, for everything you do flows from it"

- 11:13 - "A gossip betrays a confidence, but a trustworthy person keeps a secret"

- 15:22 - "Plans fail for lack of counsel, but with many advisers they succeed"

- 16:28 - "A perverse person stirs up conflict, and a gossip separates close friends"

- 18:8 - "The words of a gossip are like choice morsels; they go down to the inmost parts"

- 18:21 - "The tongue has the power of life and death, and those who love it will eat its fruit"

- 19:5 - "A false witness will not go unpunished, and whoever pours out lies will not go free"

- 22:1 - "A good name is more desirable than great riches; to be esteemed is better than silver or gold"

- 25:9-10 - "If you take your neighbor to court, do not betray another's confidence, or the one who hears it may shame you and the charge against you will stand"

- 26:20 - "Without wood a fire goes out; without a gossip a quarrel dies down"

- 27:14 - "If anyone loudly blesses their neighbor early in the morning, it will be taken as a curse"

- 27:17 - "As iron sharpens iron, so one person sharpens another"

- 3:5-6 - "Trust in the Lord with all your heart and lean not on your own understanding; in all your ways submit to him, and he will make your paths straight"

- 13:22 - "A good person leaves an inheritance for their children's children"

Ecclesiastes

- 3:11 - "He has made everything beautiful in its time"

Isaiah

- 26:3 - "You keep him in perfect peace whose mind is stayed on you, because he trusts in you"

- 30:15 - "In quietness and trust is your strength"

- 40:31 - "But those who hope in the Lord will renew their strength. They will soar on wings like eagles; they will run and not grow weary, they will walk and not be faint"

- 43:18-19 - "Forget the former things; do not dwell on the past. See, I am doing a new thing! Now it springs up; do you not perceive it? I am making a way in the wilderness and streams in the wasteland"

- 54:17 - "No weapon forged against you will prevail, and you will refute every tongue that accuses you. This is the heritage of the servants of the Lord, and this is their vindication from me, declares the Lord"

Jeremiah

- 17:9 - "The heart is deceitful above all things and beyond cure. Who can understand it?"

- 29:11 - "For I know the plans I have for you," declares the Lord, "plans to prosper you and not to harm you, to give you hope and a future"

- 31:3 - "The Lord appeared to us in the past, saying: 'I have loved you with an everlasting love; I have drawn you with unfailing kindness'"

Zephaniah

- 3:17 - "The Lord your God is with you, the Mighty Warrior who saves. He will take great delight in you; in his love he will no longer rebuke you, but will rejoice over you with singing"

New Testament

Matthew

- 5:16 - "Let your light shine before others, that they may see your good deeds and glorify your Father in heaven"

- 6:14-15 - "For if you forgive other people when they sin against you, your heavenly Father will also forgive you. But if you do not forgive others their sins, your Father will not forgive your sins"

- 7:6 - "Do not give dogs what is sacred; do not throw your pearls to pigs. If you do, they may trample them under their feet, and turn and tear you to pieces"

- 7:24 - "Therefore everyone who hears these words of mine and puts them into practice is like a wise man who built his house on the rock"

- 10:16 - "Be as shrewd as snakes and as innocent as doves"

- 11:28 - "Come to me, all you who are weary and burdened, and I will give you rest"

- 12:25 - "Every kingdom divided against itself will be ruined, and every city or household divided against itself will not stand"

- 12:34-35 - "For the mouth speaks what the heart is full of. A good man brings good things out of the good stored up in him, and an evil man brings evil things out of the evil stored up in him"

- 18:15 - "If your brother or sister sins, go and point out their fault, just between the two of you. If they listen to you, you have won them over"

Mark

- 11:25 - "And when you stand praying, if you hold anything against anyone, forgive them, so that your Father in heaven may forgive you your sins"

Luke

- 12:48 - "From everyone who has been given much, much will be demanded; and from the one who has been entrusted with much, much more will be asked"

- 17:3-4 - "So watch yourselves. If your brother or sister sins against you, rebuke them; and if they repent, forgive them. Even if they sin against you seven times in a day and seven times come back to you saying 'I repent,' you must forgive them"

- 23:34 - "Father, forgive them, for they do not know what they are doing"

John

- 8:32 - "Then you will know the truth, and the truth will set you free"

- 8:44 - "You belong to your father, the devil, and you want to carry out your father's desires. He was a murderer from the beginning, not holding to the truth, for there is no truth in him. When he lies, he speaks his native language, for he is a liar and the father of lies"

- 10:27-28 - "My sheep listen to my voice; I know them, and they follow me. I give them eternal life, and they shall never perish; no one will snatch them out of my hand"

- 14:27 - "Peace I leave with you; my peace I give you. I do not give to you as the world gives. Do not let your hearts be troubled and do not be afraid"

Romans

- 5:8 - "But God demonstrates his own love for us in this: While we were still sinners, Christ died for us"

- 8:1 - "Therefore, there is now no condemnation for those who are in Christ Jesus"

- 8:28 - "And we know that in all things God works for the good of those who love him, who have been called according to his purpose"

- 8:37 - "No, in all these things we are more than conquerors through him who loved us"

- 12:18 - "If it is possible, as far as it depends on you, live at peace with everyone"

1 Corinthians

- 13:7 - "It always protects, always trusts, always hopes, always perseveres"

2 Corinthians

- 4:1-2 - "Therefore, having this ministry by the mercy of God, we do not lose heart. But we have renounced disgraceful, underhanded ways. We refuse to practice cunning or to tamper with God's word, but by the open statement of the truth we would commend ourselves to everyone's conscience in the sight of God"

- 5:7 - "For we live by faith, not by sight"

- 5:17 - "Therefore, if anyone is in Christ, the new creation has come: The old has gone, the new is here!"

- 6:14 - "Do not be yoked together with unbelievers. For what do righteousness and wickedness have in common? Or what fellowship can light have with darkness?"

- 10:5 - "We demolish arguments and every pretension that sets itself up against the knowledge of God, and we take captive every thought to make it obedient to Christ"

Galatians

- 5:22-23 - "But the fruit of the Spirit is love, joy, peace, forbearance, kindness, goodness, faithfulness, gentleness and self-control. Against such things there is no law"

- 6:1 - "Brothers and sisters, if someone is caught in a sin, you who live by the Spirit should restore that person gently. But watch yourselves, or you also may be tempted"

- 6:2 - "Carry each other's burdens, and in this way you will fulfill the law of Christ"

Ephesians

- 1:4 - "For he chose us in him before the creation of the world to be holy and blameless in his sight"

- 1:6 - "to the praise of his glorious grace, which he has freely given us in the One he loves"

- 2:10 - "For we are God's handiwork, created in Christ Jesus to do good works, which God prepared in advance for us to do"

- 3:20-21 - "Now to him who is able to do immeasurably more than all we ask or imagine, according to his power that is at work within us, to him be glory in the church and in Christ Jesus throughout all generations, for ever and ever! Amen"

- 4:26-27 - "In your anger do not sin: Do not let the sun go down while you are still angry, and do not give the devil a foothold"

- 4:29 - "Do not let any unwholesome talk come out of your mouths, but only what is helpful for building others up according to their needs, that it may benefit those who listen"

- 4:31-32 - "Get rid of all bitterness, rage and anger, brawling and slander, along with every form of malice. Be kind and compassionate to one another, forgiving each other, just as in Christ God forgave you"

- 4:32 - "Be kind and compassionate to one another, forgiving each other, just as in Christ God forgave you"

- 6:14 - "Stand firm then, with the belt of truth buckled around your waist"

- 6:14 - "with the breastplate of righteousness in place"

- 6:15 - "and with your feet fitted with the readiness that comes from the gospel of peace"

- 6:16 - "In addition to all this, take up the shield of faith, with which you can extinguish all the flaming arrows of the evil one"

- 6:17 - "Take the helmet of salvation and the sword of the Spirit, which is the word of God"

Philippians

- 1:6 - "Being confident of this, that he who began a good work in you will carry it on to completion until the day of Christ Jesus"

- 4:6-7 - "Do not be anxious about anything, but in every situation, by prayer and petition, with thanksgiving, present your requests to God. And the peace of God, which transcends all understanding, will guard your hearts and your minds in Christ Jesus"

- 4:8 - "Finally, brothers and sisters, whatever is true, whatever is noble, whatever is right, whatever is pure, whatever is lovely, whatever is admirable—if anything is excellent or praiseworthy—think about such things"

- 4:13 - "I can do all this through him who gives me strength"

Colossians

- 3:13 - "Bear with each other and forgive one another if any of you has a grievance against someone. Forgive as the Lord forgave you"

1 Thessalonians

- 5:11 - "Therefore encourage one another and build each other up, just as in fact you are doing"

- 5:18 - "Give thanks in all circumstances; for this is God's will for you in Christ Jesus"

2 Timothy

- 1:7 - "For God has not given us a spirit of fear, but of power, of love and of sound mind"

Titus

- 3:10 - "Warn a divisive person once, and then warn them a second time. After that, have nothing to do with them"

Hebrews

- 4:12 - "For the word of God is alive and active. Sharper than any double-edged sword, it penetrates even to dividing soul and spirit, joints and marrow; it judges the thoughts and attitudes of the heart"

- 10:23 - "Let us hold unswervingly to the hope we profess, for he who promised is faithful"

- 10:24 - "And let us consider how we may spur one another on toward love and good deeds"

James

- 1:2-4 - "Consider it pure joy, my brothers and sisters, whenever you face trials of many kinds, because you know that the testing of your faith produces perseverance. Let perseverance finish its work so that you may be mature and complete, not lacking anything"

- 5:16 - "Therefore confess your sins to each other and pray for each other so that you may be healed. The prayer of a righteous person is powerful and effective"

1 Peter

- 2:9 - "But you are a chosen people, a royal priesthood, a holy nation, God's special possession, that you may declare the praises of him who called you out of darkness into his wonderful light"

- 5:7 - "Cast all your anxiety on him because he cares for you"

1 John

- 1:9 - "If we confess our sins, he is faithful and just and will forgive us our sins and purify us from all unrighteousness"

- 3:1 - "See what great love the Father has lavished on us, that we should be called children of God! And that is what we are!"

Lea Cole discovered firsthand how devastating workplace gossip and toxic communication can be when what should have been an exciting career opportunity became a battle for survival. After months of character assassination and isolation, she embarked on a healing journey that transformed not only her own life but her understanding of how to create healthier environments for others.

Through this challenging season, Lea gained invaluable wisdom about the power of words—both the destructive force of gossip and the healing power of truth. Her experience taught her that protection comes not just from avoiding toxic people, but from knowing whose voice to follow when chaos surrounds you.

Now Lea helps others navigate similar challenges through writing that combines biblical wisdom with practical strategies. Her approach addresses both what we say about others and how we protect ourselves from harmful communication patterns.

Lea believes that no one should have to face toxic communication alone. That transformation is possible for both individuals and organizations willing to choose truth over rumors and healing over harm.

www.ingramcontent.com/pod-product-compliance
Lightning Source LLC
Chambersburg PA
CBHW060423130626
46555CB00005B/2185